(0781) 74636A

Benjamin Goodall Symon, Jr.

Ben Symon in Edinburgh in October 1957

Benjamin Goodall Symon, Jr.

HIS BIOGRAPHY AND LETTERS

By

LOWELL RUSSELL DITZEN

In Collaboration with

ELIZABETH CARTER SYMON

AMHERST COLLEGE PRESS

AMHERST · MASSACHUSETTS

MCMLXIII

Introduction

I T WAS December 20, 1957. The telephone rang in my study to bring the sad and shocking news that Benjamin Goodall Symon, Jr., with his friend and fellow student, George Stebbins Moses, had just been killed in an automobile accident on the outskirts of London.

Within a few moments I was in touch with his father and mother who were in the South. As I was the first person to speak to them after the fateful word from England, I felt the full outpouring of their loss. In this I deeply shared, as did hundreds of others, when the news was spread abroad.

As I hung up the receiver, an inner voice, that has repeated itself often, was saying: "Something must be done to let the widest possible circle of young people and adults know this inspiring young man."

Ben Symon was superbly gifted scholastically, musically, socially, athletically, aesthetically, theologically. The hallmark of "excellence" was stamped on all his ventures.

He was a seeker, asking the deepest questions, voicing his doubts, yet sticking to what he found to be best. Though he had an obsession for "The Truth," he responded exuberantly to life. He laughed much and played hard.

Dozens of young people whispered through their tears, "He was my very best friend." Many of mature age said, "Ben always made me feel I was something special."

To those who cry about barnyard behavior in today's young people, Ben Symon can be pointed out as an eagle.

In my ministry in The Reformed Church of Bronxville, New York, covering more than a decade, I never saw the nave so crowded for a funeral. Adults and young people stood solemnly in the balcony and vestibule after all the pews were filled.

Trying to speak to their hurt and questioning I said: ". . . though Benjamin Goodall's life was limited in terms of quantity, it has been magnificent in terms of *quality*. Life is to be measured not in its length, but in its capacity to respond—to grow—to give."

Several key thoughts were the subject of long debate with his schoolmates and the cause for deep introspection. One of those friends of high school days, Barbara Hanna, felt there were certain affirmations Ben stated early in life that continued in his search of the ensuing years:

1. The quest for truth is one of the most important tasks to which a man can give his thought and energy.

2. The greatest challenge of life is to find certainty in a world of doubt.

3. One never "becomes a Christian" but one is always "becoming."

4. A basic and ever-present personal problem is "to correlate the doubtful mind and the hopeful soul into a state of common agreement and reciprocal confirmation."

5. One of the purposes of life is to "touch people," to know them, to understand them, to let the best in your life reach out to the best in theirs.

6. The joy of life is to recognize and appreciate "pure moments." Ben's reading, travel, and concern for all kinds of people gave him such "pure moments." He spoke and wrote of them and held them as truest treasures.

Many who knew him may not have had occasion to learn of these intimate thoughts of young Ben. But without exception all admired his character and accomplishments.

Typical is the following evaluation from Albert L. Williams, Executive Vice-President of International Business Machines Corporation, recommending Ben for study abroad:

November 9, 1956

Dear Sir:

Ben Symon is a young man of outstanding character, high intelligence, and, in my opinion is a born leader with a great understanding of people from different backgrounds. He had a fine academic record, was president of the Student Council and of the

Young People's Group at his Church. This in addition to taking an active interest in athletics, music, and other affairs of the school and community.

Ben has the unusual quality of standing for the good and fine things of life without appearing to be "goody-goody" and, as a result, exercises a constructive influence in whatever he enters. I have had occasion to spend some time abroad and know of no young man I would have more confidence in as representing the United States in a way we would all be proud to claim.

Ben liked competent writing. His mother recalls an occasion when he was reading Anne Lindbergh's *Gift of the Sea*. Closing the book, he exclaimed: "The power of words—both written and spoken! But it is the written word that just fascinates me. This book—well—you've just got to read it, Mother! It's such beautiful writing."

Much of Ben's own writing was in the form of hurried notes probably intended only for his own eyes. These, together with his letters and papers, are cited freely in the following pages, without editing; only in some instances individual names are deleted.

The dedication of this book is to Ben's parents, Mr. and Mrs. Benjamin Goodall Symon, Sr. Now living in Daphne, Alabama, they have given this project their continuous and generous concern. Mrs. Symon devoted many hours to recording incidents in her son's life and, with Mr. Symon, was indefatigable in gathering and transcribing Ben's letters, notes, and papers.

Their love is in this book for a son who loved them and loves them still.

Miss Patricia Stauffer, Mrs. Orden Oechsli, Mrs. M. P. Hubbard, Mrs. Virginia Klein, and Mrs. Arch Crawford have given time, skill, and concern in typing and editing.

A verse of scripture that Ben couldn't escape was, "You have not chosen me, but I have chosen you." Those words intrigued him from early adolescence. They caused him to ponder time and again, "Who am I? What is my life work to be? What am I chosen to do?"

His mother, a deeply spiritual and radiant person, sensed:

"A Power that planted in his mind high ideals and a will to strive for their attainment, that stirred his soul in communion with art, music, and great literature; a Power that made his heart feel the receiving of love in the giving of love, that flooded his

face with joy in sharing the joy of others, that made him sensitive
to the burdens of others, that prompted him to offer a listening
ear or a helping hand; a Power that made him hungry for truth,
that gave him energy for his tasks, that ruled out idleness or bore-
dom; a Power that regarded the bonds of family and home as a
sacred trust, that bowed his head in reverent worship and in deep
humility for any praise; a Power that gave him a faith in God
and in his fellow man and which made the serving of both his
supreme purpose in life."

It is now six years since Ben Symon was killed. Yet his goodness
lives on. As you come to know him, I think he will add gladness
and depth to your life, as he did to us who knew him.

Into the circle of friendship with this admirable spirit, you are
invited.

LOWELL RUSSELL DITZEN

"Arrivederci"
Cold Brook, New York
November 21, 1963

CONTENTS

Foreword

THIS RECORD of the life of an entirely fine young man will be particularly moving for those of us who knew him and have stared helplessly at the arbitrary fact of his early death. The book has great intrinsic interest as the record of what a positive and joyful thing a life can be, in a period when so many lives are vitiated, contorted, or wasted. For those who are concerned with what actually happens in college, it is both an illuminating and a heartening document. As a chapter in the history of Amherst College in particular, Ben Symon's account of his undergraduate experience in the mid-twentieth century is comparable to the mid-nineteenth-century account which is furnished us by the college diaries of Judge William Gardiner Hammond, edited by George F. Whicher. In view of what we often assume about the distraction, dissipation, and dismay of contemporary undergraduates, it is reassuring to find how much in common there is between Symon's life at Amherst and Hammond's: both participated in urgent undergraduate discussions of fundamental problems, both performed literary exercises, both took part in organizing social and intellectual events, both formed deep friendships, both enjoyed the country and a good measure of undergraduate fun. One gets the impression that the serious side of college life was much more of a routine for the nineteenth-century undergraduate than it was for Symon's generation—and so perhaps not really quite so serious. But this difference is in part a reflection of the two different men: Symon was a deeper person than Hammond, responsible to a larger capacity for doubt and growth. By the same token, he was less typical, probably, of his generation; we cannot, unfortunately, point to his college experience as a norm for his time. But it is splendid that such living and learning *is* a possibility and that he realized the possibility.

When I was directing his senior thesis on Yeats, he would come in for the weekly conference with an unselfconscious bustle, *just* on time, with an armful of marked books and the draft of part of the text hot from the oven; he would plunge in at once, intense and yet diffident. His ruddy, firmly featured face (from which one got a sense of strong bones, a sturdy prow) would be closed most of the time in concentration, opening into humor and fun only at intervals. It was hard to be sure, at first, that this would not be a somewhat awkward student, clumsy on the turns; his delicacy and subtlety came out gradually. But it became clear that he was coming to Yeats with important questions about art and experience— as I can see more clearly now in reading his letters and excerpts from his other student papers.

What he did in his thesis was to take seriously the early explorations by Yeats, in his "poetical" first poetry, of art as a kind of revelation, and then to show that the same fundamental view of art is *also* characteristic of the greater and more popular "antipoetic" poetry of his maturity. He brought to his study of Yeats some real experience of this function of poetry as it was developed by the French symbolists from Baudelaire—knowledge acquired by his work in France and with Professor Elmo Giordanetti. Behind was his own concern for "pure moments" of perception (described at the opening of Chapter III and in several of the letters) together with his own experience of faith: "not something gained and maintained on an even level . . ." but coming "in instants, not once, but many times, and in different ways, and under many different circumstances." (p. 55.) But his personal experience was never the subject of our conferences or of his writing in the thesis; his eye was always on the object, on the poems, the criticism, the poetic tradition; the life behind the eye found expression in what the eye saw. And so what he produced was disciplined criticism. That it was the best criticism produced that year by an undergraduate English major was ground for great satisfaction. But still more important was the integrity of life and work which it exemplified.

His integrity, in all relations, was what especially distinguished him—not any one of his remarkable talents, but his responsibility to them, his wholeness. And his integrity was not maintained defensively, by exclusion. Ben Symon was in many ways an old-fashioned person. Coming up to Amherst, he might have retreated into self-righteous isolation; instead he entered actively into undergraduate life, communicating with contemporaries whose mentality and attitudes towards life differed, in various ways, from his own. About fraternity life, for example, his letters describe both the silly, mean, and messy things, and also the camaraderie, friendship, and freedom which can develop—the "study" made in the house attic, out of scrap wood and hardboard and two electric heaters; the $40-refrigerator financed at $10, pro rata, "a two-year investment." His extra-ordinary quality, because it did not exclude the ordinary, makes this book at once a record of mid-twentieth-century experience at Amherst, and a critique of it.

Because this book includes an account of what Ben Symon came to Amherst from, and of the first opening out of his horizons after he left and went to Edinburgh, it makes clear how the life and learning in a college depends on the quality of the lives that flow through it. His own life, centered as it was in the strength that came from religious experience and commitment, makes us aware of another flow, coming in from outside particular antecedents, and effective beyond particular terminations.

C. L. BARBER
Professor of English

Bloomington, Indiana
October 1, 1963

Benjamin Goodall Symon, Jr.

Biographical Notes

THE ANCESTRAL origins of Benjamin Goodall Symon, Jr. are linked with the British Isles, particularly Scotland.

Ben's mother, born Elizabeth Carter at Troy, Alabama, was the daughter of Sarah Johnson Crossley and Tyree Shelby Carter. His father, Benjamin Goodall Symon, Sr., was born in Brookfield, Missouri. In the family lines, whether traced in Scotland, Ireland, or America, there are clergymen, doctors, teachers, and farmers. All were marked as hardy people with a capacity for work and a doggedness in fulfilling their responsibility. They had a stalwart faith in God, intellectual integrity, and a concern for their fellow men. Those traits are exemplified in the lives of the two people whose second son was born on June 6, 1935 and who was baptized Benjamin Goodall Symon, Jr.

The first five years for their active, reddish-haired boy were spent in Webster Groves, a suburb of St. Louis, Missouri. Then a year in Bronxville, New York and an interlude till age ten in New Rochelle, returning to Bronxville, where the family lived until 1960.

Marks of character were emerging through his grade school life: courage, humility, loyalty, integrity, modesty, simplicity, perseverance.

As president of his Elementary School Council, Ben presided over a meeting that heatedly discussed the question of a student council motto and badge. The school Principal, present as advisor, finally said, "Mr. President, what do you have to say?"

Ben stood. "Well, I've been listening and thinking, and the way I feel about it is—if we do our job well, we won't need a motto or badge. We'll be known by the kind of job we do."

Telling of the incident later, the Principal said, "I'll defy a trained executive to resolve a problem more ably than that! That lad thrills me!"

His enthusiasm was great for parties and dances. He wasn't sure at first about the traditional "Miss Covington's dancing classes." After his first lesson, he was asked what he learned. Scratching his head he answered quizzically, "Let me think—she called it—the O-x—? —Yes, the Ox-trot!" But shortly, like all activities, it was great "fun," and Ben became one of Miss Covington's demonstrating dancers for parental observation.

Although the Symon boys had a weekly allowance, they were taught to put aside one-tenth for Sunday School collection. As Ben expanded his financial enterprises by working for neighbors, the Scottish sense of stewardship prevailed. He kept a small notebook showing three columns labeled "earned," "spent," and "good causes." Under the last was a long list of contributions to school, Church, and community. He kept a diary, for a time, in which he occasionally mentioned difficulty in collecting loans from hard-pressed pals.

A surprise party, which his parents gave for Ben on his eighteenth birthday, included his classmates and his teachers. It was on Sunday afternoon and had been planned not to interfere with Ben's responsibility as President of the Youth Fellowship at his Church. Many lingered on, after refreshments, chatting and laughing on the lawn and terrace. As it neared six o'clock Ben disappeared, then returned with his Bible in hand. "I'm sorry to have to leave. You were all good to come. Please don't rush, but I must leave to keep an appointment." Then with a "So long, I'll be seeing you," he dashed to the Church.

Amherst College was entered with enthusiasm. He made the Glee Club in his freshman year and was later chosen for the Chapel Choir, a screened group of more capable voices which develop a repertoire for all chapel services. At the end of his freshman year he was named to replace a graduating senior in the Amherst "DQ" or double quartet. Though these three musical groups required many hours of rehearsal, Ben participated in them fully during the four college years. Concerts were given locally and on various tours to Bermuda, throughout New England, the Mid-West, and South.

He early joined the Christian Association and participated in the worship services, discussions, and the planning for religious affairs on the college campus.

To get an answer to the question, "Who am I?," and the meaning of the scriptural verse, "Ye have not chosen me, but I have chosen you," Ben attended several conferences at Union Theological Seminary in New York for prospective candidates for the ministry. Both the academic and spiritual side of these conferences he found stimulating. He discussed endlessly the wide field of religion and the life of the spirit with friends and associates.

His mother recalls a night during a holiday when one of Ben's favorite college friends was visiting. The boys were engaged in scholarly talk when she said goodnight to them around midnight. She was awakened after 2:00 A.M. by what seemed violent disagreements. It was obvious from Ben's rising voice that this was no lukewarm conversation. Listening in the hall and hearing that the argument had to do with the reality of God, Mrs. Symon quietly and thankfully returned to her own rest.

One of Ben's favorite songs was Debussy's "La Mer." His fraternity brothers knew he was home at the day's end, as he sang or hummed it climbing the stairs to his third-floor room, or paused to play it at the piano. "La Mer" was still with him when later he went to Edinburgh, where it was played first in the frequent evening "concerts" before the nightly studying.

Often, to the surprise of friends, he would pause in single-minded concentration at any lovely or meaningful thing. It might be a sunset, the lingering notes of music, or the glistening magic of ice-encrusted trees. Ben became withdrawn and quiet at such times. He said that these moments "hit to the base of my soul, and I want them to make a permanent impression there." He added that when he was tired or depressed these recollections returned the wonder of the original experience and gave a spiritual lift.

Ben felt everyone was exposed to such hallowed moments, but sadly, "many people forget to remember them."

Three times during his college days Ben left his studies to go home with some friend when there was death in the family. On one occasion, a neighbor and father of one of his high school friends died. Ben, up early to study, noticed the announcement of the death and hour of the funeral in a day-old paper. Having quickly changed his clothes, he headed for Bonxville arriving in time to spend a few minutes with his friend before going to the Church. Later to his parents he explained, "When I saw the announcement I realized you were away and our friends needed us.

I just had to get there!"

Among his papers was an unfinished letter to Dr. Ronald Mc-Neur, Assistant Minister of our church with whom Ben was closely associated. In it he expressed his desire for a place where he could be silent and alone. When he came home for vacation, anticipating an opportunity to read quietly, innumerable friends and social events interrupted.

There was compensation for this in his striking ability to concentrate. Ben could become so fully absorbed in music, drawing, or reading that he was oblivious to all else. Still he spoke of wanting "some isolated spot," perhaps with a close friend, where one can "think through a lot of things disturbing our minds and sort out our thoughts. There just isn't enough undisturbed time at school or at home either." He did get some quiet during spring vacation when a troublesome knee, injured in high school football, was given necessary surgery. Those convalescent hours were spent in reading and reflection.

The following press notice at Amherst shows one of the many ways he shared in college and fraternity life:

> 1955 . . . Benjamin G. Symon, Jr., an Amherst Junior from Bronxville, N. Y., is in charge of the religious discussion groups in his fraternity. Nine noted Church leaders will conduct the two day program. . . . The current topic, "Rebels and Responsible Men," will be the focal point of evening sessions.

By Christmastime of that year, he told his family he had determined to carry on his studies in a Seminary. His parents were moved; it was a solemn moment for them, as it was for Ben.

Before serving the traditional Christmas dinner in the Symon household and the lighting of candles, it was customary to have a short reading or meditation as a variation of the usual daily table blessing. As his mother asked him to lead, Ben read John 3:19-21 and II Corinthians 4:4-6. Then he spoke of the "Light of Christ" in the human heart, adding that the hope of mankind depended on the Light from the Gospel of Christ. He then lit his candle and each individual in turn lit his or hers from the person next until the circle of light went around the table.

Trips to Europe, his impressions of people, his questions and concerns, are revealed through his own letters and papers in the following pages.

And it is through them one finds him—a very delightful young man.

CHAPTER 1

Through High School

THOSE WHO knew Ben as a small child were struck with his energy and imagination. Observing his enthusiasm and capacity for absorption, a neighbor, who was a Biblical scholar, exclaimed, "If Goodall should ever use that energy for God's ministry, what a power he will be!"

His kindergarten teacher's first report read:

> Goodall is a most delightful pupil. His enthusiasm and fine spirit of cooperation make him a leader in our group. He shows a natural talent for art and music.

First grade report:

> Steadily growing ability; takes great pride in his work; does his very best with the job at hand; his intelligent questions contribute much to group discussion.

Ben's boyhood delight with Christmas never waned, though its significance deepened across the years. He wrote in uncertain second grade script to Santa Claus, enclosing an advertisement of a "football helmet, $1.79." After requesting "this helmet," a special book, and two or three smaller toys, the letter ended: "and anything else you think is right."

A year later the annual letter read:

> Dear Santa:
> Will you please Bring me some Books, the names of the Books are Lassie come Home, 4 Hardy Boys. Man from Music Mountain. And a machine gun, and a football and whatever else you think is right.
>
> Goodall Symon.

Placed in an experimental class for gifted children, his fifth and sixth grade teachers reported:

5

He knows how to work with concentration and power, hence he improves steadily. He has growing personal standards for his accomplishment. The library habit is well developed and book choices show a maturing taste. He has read seventeen books this semester.

When I criticize his work he is quick to recognize his own weaknesses. . . .

Later a Junior High School classmate recalls:

An incident took place that has remained in my mind as symbolic of Ben's strong will and character. We were playing a game of basketball one afternoon. Ben was in possession of the ball and had a clear court in front of him, but in his anxiety he missed the shot. He threw his arms out wildly, stamped the floor in disgust, and gave out with a loud "fiddlesticks." I laugh whenever I think back on that incident but at the same time it was one of many things that never failed to impress me about Ben.

Ben began early to write letters to relatives and friends. A letter to his grandmother written when he was fifteen read:

Dear Grandmother:

I know you are getting tired of that hospital and we're getting tired of having you in it too. But just keep up the good work and and you'll soon be out. . . .

I'm applying for my driver's license now and I hope to have it by August. . . .

Last Sunday we went into the city to Fifth Avenue Presbyterian Church and heard Dr. MacDonald, visiting minister from Scotland. He preached a fine Sermon—logical and concise, applying Christian ideals and principles to the problems of today's world. He was easy to follow and I thoroughly enjoyed hearing him. . . .

We're all thinking about you every day, pulling for you, praying for you.

All the love in this world,
Goodall

The following portion of a paper written during high school shows his growing preoccupation with religion:

Religion is the only hope of the world today. The building up of a faith within the minds and hearts of people throughout the world is the only way to avoid feelings of skepticism, fear and suspicion. This faith must transcend political or secular affiliations. It must be a faith in the dignity and destiny of all mankind.

It must be a faith that reaches out into all the world and claims the allegiance of all men to a belief in the existence of a Supreme Being—originator of all Creation.

A classmate wrote of him:

We played ball together, went to dancing school together, and graduated together. During all these years right from grade school, he was an example to the rest of us.

Most of all I will remember him for his constant reflection on Good, his search for a belief that he could live by sincerely. That to me is the sign of a truly fine person—a person who can put that good above the emphasis on materialism.

His ideals will live on as cherished memories—vital, soothing, strengthening.

Football was curtailed due to damaged cartilage in the knee, but there was a surging ahead in other fields. To a studio recital given by Ben, his piano teacher invited her own New York teacher, an outstanding musician, who followed with this note:

The Symon lad has genuine talent and reveals a sincere love for the instrument and the score. Be thankful that he, and through reflection, we too can gain so much by his industry and talent. . . .

Ben and his friends moved into the production of amateur movies with Ben as "experienced" camera man. They made a colored film of "Lee's Surrender to Grant," ransacking attics for heirloom uniforms. Adding modern versions of Yankee and Confederate caps, troops were outfitted—doing their performance on a vacant lot. The result greatly intrigued the boys and there were as many reviews of the picture as of the football games. Other "productions" included "an Arab Battle," staged at Jones Beach, with their mothers' towels and sheets as costumes. At the Reformed Church Ben had a part in making an unusually fine motion picture portraying the life of Martin Luther.

Excerpts from a couple of his science papers reflect the depth of his approach to this subject:

Time and Space
THE IONOSPHERE

We could not fully appreciate the significance of the ionosphere until we had studied it and and so come to understand it. From this, we may logically conclude that true understanding leads to practical appreciation. . . . if more people could only acquire such a spirit of appreciation for the many things that they take for granted, what a better world this would be, for a practical or positive appreciation is the cornerstone of wisdom!

Apparent Motion
SUN, MOON, AND PLANETS

Man, by his very nature, is an inquisitive creature. His curiosity entices him on his road of civilized progression. . . .

Man, again by his very nature, is a profoundly self-centered creature. Because of this, there often is a tendency to seek knowledge and truth, not for their own sake, but for the sake of self-interest and self-justification. . . . So we see that the mind of man has been the field of battle for two basic human traits: natural curiosity and self-centered egotism.

The Ptolemaic System, proposed in the second century A.D. . . . with its progressive complexity and increasing unmanageableness, lasted for 1500 years before it was even challenged! Yet, after the initial step had been taken by Copernicus, our modern theory evolved into an accepted and proven fact in less than 300 years. Why? Because men were convinced they possessed final knowledge and ultimate truth. They were forgetting that there is no final knowledge; for each new discovery leads to new fields of thought. . . . We must continually seek after knowledge and truth, and if we seek, we shall find. But the process is never ending.

He was chosen "athlete of the week" for Westchester County. News and editorials read:

Bronxville High's Coach Dan Matthaei called Ben Symon one of the most unselfish athletes he had ever met. "You don't find many like Ben. He's a fine athlete . . . and could have had a letter in basketball this season if he hadn't injured his knee in football. He is one of the fastest boys we have in the school . . . has a fine mind, a top student. While he's scoring a basketball game he remembers where the shots are being missed and made from.

The Sports Editor wrote:

Each week the Con Edison people present a "Sports Award" to an outstanding athlete in Westchester County who by his action exemplifies all that is fine in the whole man, the athlete who is a classic example in good sportmanship. It must be a person connected with sports who is a great champion. Last week in Bronxville Con Edison made an excellent choice and this scribe adds his name to those who picked Ben Symon for the award. . . .

As far as being the outstanding athlete at Bronxville, the choice might go elsewhere; but as far as being the popular choice for the Con Edison Award and what it means, that belongs to Ben Symon. At the football banquet, young Ben played the piano as only Ben could do. Playing the piano may be an avocation to Ben but it could be a career. When Ben finished and the whole squad gave a cheer, Sports-caster Russ Hodges turned to us and remarked, "Now that's the kind of a football player I like!"

It was a custom for *The Mirror*, the local high school paper, to run an article on each senior. Of Ben:

. . . When told by the doctor that the sudden jerks and stops he would have to make in baseball might throw his knee out again, he switched to track and got his varsity letter, running the 880. His best time was a fine 2:09.

Came the football season of his senior year, Ben was at it once more. In the last scrimmage before the first game, it happened again—out went his knee. His knee strong enough now, Ben is back on the baseball diamond, holding down the varsity third base position.

No one deserves more credit for coming back against tough breaks and showing really great athletic ability than Ben Symon.

A paper written in his senior year on the subject "Materialism vs. Spiritualism" shows his thinking:

Man should mold his character around a simple but closely knit core of fundamental, moral, and ethical beliefs. This will insure for him the construction of a character which will undergo the most taxing tests of crisis and change. . . .

The attainment of such a state is not easy. Life is too complex and too merciless in its judgment for any man to completely overcome its temptations and hazards. . . .

Materialism has become the dominant force in our society; it guides us both in our business and in our government. . . . We seem to have forgotten that there is no substitute for truth, for honor, or for personal integrity. We have tried to substitute security for these things, and we are just beginning to find out its shortcomings. . . . Rome was doomed but we still have within us the means to save ourselves. What is needed is a resurgence of spiritual consciousness and a re-dedication to the guidance of this consciousness.

> The strongest bulwark against materialistic trends is the building up and maintenance of a strong character, based on fundamental beliefs in the existence of God, and in the omnipotent force of love for one's God and for one's fellow man. We must reaffirm our purpose. . . . We must begin to look for the right and, what is far greater, we must begin to *do* the right.

All of his serious thoughts were not confined to class papers. In his social gatherings there was discussion of moral matters with Ben often leading the conversation.

At the Memorial Day student body gathering of 1953 Ben spoke:

> As we come together and commemorate the sacrifices of these men and women, we are trying to create inspiration to hold high the ideals of freedom for which they fought so valiantly. . . . We are trying to create determination to guard these ideals, each and every one of us, within our own minds and hearts. If we could walk away from this ceremony with this feeling in us, not just on Memorial Day, but on all days, we could be sure that our freedom would never die.

Ben's Senior Yearbook is filled with notes of affection from his fellow students:

> To Ben—the greatest guy and Prexy B. H. S. ever had.
> Ben—B. H. S. will miss one of its outstanding presidents. Continue your terrific work and you will write a glowing chapter in Amherst's records.
> Pal, you were great!
> Ben—the greatest guy to get things done!
> I'd never have made it without you! From Fifth Grade to Class Day, it's been great! Best of luck for next year.
> I'll never forget this year—the operetta, blasts, profound talks, etc., would never have been without you.
> It's been wonderful knowing you and loving you all these years! As far as I'm concerned leaving you means more tears for me than anyone else—love always.
> To the greatest guy. I enjoyed doing things with you and hope to continue the friendship for ever.
> We've had one great time since 5th grade! My love always.

Later a vacation Bible School teacher wrote more fully to Mr. and Mrs. Symon:

There was everything admirable and promising as well as endearing about Goodall. He had found purpose and direction in his life because of his wonderful Christian family life, fine education and keen mind. In a world of so many young men out to "get" from life, he was willing and eager to "give."

My deepest love to you both.

D.

The summer of 1953 was an adventure of classmates determined to have a "work experience" on Cape Cod. Some of Ben's letters to his parents, telling of the summer's vicissitudes, include:

c/o Howard Johnson's Restaurant
Orleans, Massachusetts
June 30, 1953

Fred's car broke down somewhere around Middlebury, Conn., on the Merritt Parkway. Just what happened, I'm not sure, as I haven't heard directly from either of them.

All four of us are in a *small* cabin with two double decker beds —space is about 20 by 15—(did I say small!??). It's not too bad . . . yet. I just hope we don't get tired of it.

Crawf and George are working behind the fountain, whereas Jack and I are in the kitchen.

Mother, about swimming on Plymouth Beach, etc. Don't worry, we'll be careful.

Chatham, Mass.
July 10, 1953

As for money, I have $6 after paying $10 for two weeks rent. This should last me through Sunday when I'll receive a fat pay check (I'm working a 7-day week this week and expect about $38 pay).

Tell Grandmother I met an old Scotch tailor up here (he must be at least 85). He talks with a brogue and is really quite a character.

I've got to rise and shine at 6:30 tomorrow morning, and it's already 12:30. . . . Tell Joanna [a visiting little cousin who presented a bit of a problem with the TV] to watch her Ps and Qs and let the TV set cool off once in a while.

Love,
Goodie

Chatham, Mass.
July 19, 1953

Dear Mother and Dadden:

I just got back from church—Methodist—only a block from our new place.

Jack and I have been working in a laundry—a big company which hauls in about $15,000 a week from all the camps and big inns all over the Cape.

Now about where we are staying. By a stroke of extremely good fortune we've found an ideal spot—almost too good to be true. We're situated right in Chatham proper—convenient to all the restaurants and shops. This will save us plenty of gas (I do believe Crawf's car is giving us about 5 miles a gallon). We have a large room over a garage—the owner has a big placard on the front edifice with his name inscribed in huge gold letters—HORATIO HALL.

I've got $20 in the bank and I've been doing a little scrimping to keep it there. I don't get my $36 from the laundry until tomorrow. Meals up here are really expensive.

I know that you'll probably raise the argument that I could get plenty of outside work at home—mowing lawns, etc. But I think that just the experience of being up here for a while offsets this.

Chatham, Mass.
August 6, 1953

Now that our escapade is drawing to a close, I have to admit it will be good to be home. We've had some good experience, and I suppose it will prove worthwhile as we look back on it. But I crave a little time to relax and digest what I've learned. I feel that I am voicing the sentiments of my comarades-in-arms as well as myself.

Love,
Goodie

P.S. What a colossal coincidence. I met a fellow in the laundry the other day who went to school with Missy in Tokyo! With this I will close with the original observation—"It all goes to prove it's a small world!"

CHAPTER 2

Amherst—Freshman Year

THE FIRST LETTER from Ben to his parents from college read:

Dear Mother and Dadden:
Am in desperate straits. When I went to shave tonight, I found I'd left the cord to my electric razor hanging over the sink in my bathroom. Fortunately, I have a safety razor—but it plays havoc with my face. So if you get a chance before you leave, please send up the cord. I think I've done pretty well to have gotten away without forgetting anything else . . . !
Love,
Goodie

Three colleges had been visited, but Amherst was his unquestioned choice. "It just has to be my college! It has everything I want!" He applied to no other.

After two weeks at Amherst, a letter to his parents in London, where Mr. Symon was called on business, bubbled with enthusiasm for his roommates, new friends, classes, and campus life.

Amherst had a required physics course for freshmen which proved a Waterloo for many a promising student. Ben's mark from the first physics test was so low that he went to the Dean asking to be switched to a slower class. "Sir, there must have been some mistake. I have no science training or aptitude, yet I'm in the fast class. I've given this course all I've got, and I just don't think I can pass it."

A letter home later evidenced his relief:

I'd just gotten my physics test back and I "racked up" a C. Granted it was a low C, but it was better than I expected.
If you get a chance, please ask Mr. Davis at the Church when

13

the Choir is going to sing the Messiah and if it would be possible for me to sing in it when I get home.

Must sign off—French test tomorrow, and it's 11:30 already.

Love,
Goodie

P.S. The cookies are great—there aren't many left.

Ben's first mark of D ended a B as the final.

Mr. and Mrs. Symon told Ben to telephone home at any time. These direct conversations resulted in a limited necessity for correspondence. However, there are a few letters from the first year of college:

Amherst, February 4, 1954

Dear Mother & Dadden:

Everything is kind of settling down into the rut of daily assignments, complaining about food, getting to bed late and getting up early. The general mood can be sort of summed up by the remark one of the fellows back from his semester break: "Only seven more weeks and we'll be out for Spring Vacation."

That's just about the way everybody feels. I will say though that physics seems a little more interesting—but maybe that's because I'm at last understanding some of it. This in itself is "interesting" because of its novelty.

In the summer of 1954, a former high school teacher of history was to take a group of students (high school seniors and college freshmen) on a study tour of France and Switzerland. Because Ben had been denied camping experiences, his parents were glad to give him this opportunity. Wrote Ben:

. . . About this European proposition. I don't know why I even hesitated about a decision. . . . If you see the way clear to say "yes," I'll go only if you promise to forego any notion of a car in the next couple of years. This trip should take the place of that. I want to keep things on a fair basis—The European deal is something extra and I don't know why it shouldn't be naturally dubbed with the label "substitute." At any rate, such are my humble sentiments.

From his summer notebook came these observations:

Today dawned dismal, and after last night's party ('till 3 A.M.), I was in no condition to rouse myself for "le petit dejeuner." Last night was the culmination of a wonderful experience. We met a

great crowd of people on another tour the first night out of
N.Y., and last night we all got together for a last fling—Howard; Janice (32); Carolyn (35); Ariel (22, and cellist excellente—
an amazing girl); Dorothy (?)—good fun and a good spirit; Bob
Helmrich (those English cigarettes of his!); and Jane, one of the
finest persons I think I've ever met: a fresh awareness of life
which has a way of being contagious—graduated from U.C.L.A.
a year ago or so, now teaching in Los Angeles in an elementary
school.

Tomorrow we land at Cherbourg, then on to Paris by boat train
for the night;—looking forward to it.

*   *   *

Yesterday we slipped into Cobh, Ireland. It was twilight and
the rose-colored sky high-lighted the mellow colors of the hills—
soft yellow and green with brown mixed in. As we glided by, the
hills closed behind us, the channel narrowed, and we were able
to see houses along the shore and staggered up the hill sides. A
somber-looking fort loomed over us from a steep bluff. Sea gulls
flocked around the ship and their eerie cries filled the air. There
was no other sound. Twilight deepened into dusk, and a restful
quiet reigned over all. There was no light from the windows of
the houses, even though it was fast becoming dark.

The moon came out shedding its soft light over the scene. It
was a time for thought: it all seemed like a picture out of my
imagination— not real, and yet I knew it was real. It was good
to see.

Letters written to family members tell the story of his growing
understanding of the world about him.

Friday, July 3, 1954

Dear Mother and Dadden:

Day before yesterday we sighted an iceberg off to port and we
passed within 2 or 3 hundred yards of it. (The Captain went 120
miles out of his way so that we could see it.) It was a rather eerie
sight. I'd say about 60 feet high and about 50 or 60 yards in di-
ameter, and when you think that nine-tenths of the iceberg is
invisible beneath the surface, that's quite a hunk of ice! . . . They
had a ship talent show the other night and one of the girls played
the cello. I haven't heard anything so beautiful in a long time.
She put practically everyone in a trance. She hopes to be playing
in the L.A. Philharmonic Orchestra in a year or so when there's
an opening. While she was playing, I happened to notice the

cellist of the ship's orchestra sitting behind her (the man whose cello she was playing). He was staring off into space with tears streaming down his face. That just gives you an idea of how wonderful this girl was.

I don't know what else there is to tell except that finances are in fine shape. Oh yes, our cabin! It has no porthole and so with the light out you can't tell whether it's day or night. We call it "The Hole." But we are sleeping well and that's all that matters since that's all we use it for.

I'll write you again when we arrive in Geneva. If you get any brainstorms as to a wedding present for Bob and Langston, let me know "Toute de suite." . . . *Au Revoir.*

Love,
Goodie

Maison Internationale des Etudiants
Geneve, Switzerland
Mercredi—le triez juillet.

Mon cher Mama et Papa,

We got to Geneva yesterday and started our classes today. We are by far the worst of the students and we're going to have to work hard to get anything out of this.

We have 20 hours of classes a week. But we also have times set aside on weekends and on Wednesdays for excursions around and about the country side. We are going to buy some bicycles. We walked all day today through the whole city of Geneva—from 1 o'clock 'til 6:30 we walked—J'etait un peu fatigué. . . .

The more I see unfolding before me, the more I like it and the more interested I get. I'm trying to keep a diary of sorts—but the entries are spread apart and spontaneous. However, I figure anything I can get down on paper will help.

My room-mate is getting ready to sack out and feeling very much in sympathy with his exclamation of "je suis tres fatigué!," I'll sign off for now. . . .

Geneva, Switzerland
Wednesday, July 14, 1954

Dear Auntie Sliv and Mother Ragon:

We had a great waiter at our table named Kurt, whose talent was in feeding us more food than practically the rest of the dining room put together. Without our even asking, he brought us 3 and sometimes 4 main portions apiece—and *always* 3 or 4 desserts. We had very good food considering we were 3rd class— watermelons, cheese, good soups, etc.

I want to thank you two for that more than generous Bon Voyage note. . . . It certainly came in handy and I do appreciate it very much.

P.S. By the way, some of us were sea-sick.

> Maison Internationale des Etudiants
> Geneva, Switzerland
> Wednesday, July 21, 1954

Dear Mother and Dadden:

Remember in Geneva those statues in commemoration of Calvin and the Reformation? Well, the University is right across from them, as you probably recall, and we're living on the street right above them. . . .

We absorb as much as possible during class, but as far as homework is concerned, I'm afraid we don't do too awfully well. I'm trying to schedule myself in a "happy median" where I'll be apt to gain the most benefit. Sometimes this median is hard to find, because it's hard to decide, on the spot, what will offer the most valuable dividends. . . .

Last Saturday we went on an excursion to Lausanne and the surrounding countryside. We walked about 12 kilometres (8 or 10 miles) up and down the mountain roads. I'm hoping for some pictures, although the haze was bad. I've almost decided to invest in a haze filter for the Argus—only costs about $3 I think. Would make a big improvement on landscape shots. . . .

I'm going down tomorrow to buy a watch for myself and an alarm clock for Bob and Langston. I haven't been able to think of anything more practical which I would get good value on over here. As far as money is concerned, I'm not doing too badly. So far, I've spent about $25 all together since I hit the continent. We have to pay for cleaning and any laundry we have (which for me is confined to my Khaki trousers—i.e., unless I can borrow an iron from someone around here), and with the two watches, I imagine that will take quite a cut out of my funds. But I'm not worried, because at the rate I'm going, I should come out all right. Besides, we will be spending a lot less when we begin cycling through Brittany, etc. When you're in a big city money changes hands a lot quicker. . . .

This week-end we're off to Zermatt and the Matterhorn. It promises to be a spectacular and we will be there two days.

> Love,
> Goodie

Maison Internationale des Etudiants
Geneve, Switzerland
Tuesday, July 27, 1954

Dear Mother and Dadden:

. . . Geneva is *the* most beautiful and friendly city I have ever been in—I'm going to be sorry to leave.

We have been complaining a little about the food here at the Maison, but I think most of it is the result of some vague feeling that some complaints are necessary. . . .

I have never seen such a wonderful sight as Zermatt and the Matterhorn, and never expect to see another to equal it. We were lucky in having good weather and visibility for the two days we were there, and so we were able to see the Matterhorn and all the surrounding peaks very clearly. On Saturday we went to Gomergrat by the mountain train and had lunch there at about 10,000 feet. Then we returned to Zermatt and at the Victoria Hotel (where, by the way, we had *great* food—I had *four* helpings of meat, potatoes, etc.).

On Sunday we started hiking at 8 a.m. and didn't return til 6:45 in the evening. In the course of that time we climbed up to a mountain hotel at about 11,000 feet or so for lunch (complete with wine). After lunch we climbed higher toward the Matterhorn —all the way up to about 12,500 feet—where we could really go no further without ropes, axe, etc. At this point Peter and I climbed up a rock ledge to get a little better view and a couple of pictures. Pete, ahead of me, reached the top and pulled himself up. As he did so he found himself staring down 4,000 feet at the valley below.

We both felt mighty *small* and *insignificant* as we looked up at the Matterhorn, towering over us—and then at the valley far below. There was snow and the air was perceptibly cooler. It was all perfectly safe. There were paths all the way up to where we were. The whole two days—hotel, train rides from Geneva to Zermatt and back, etc.—cost 80 francs per person, or about $20.

Mother, you'll be interested to know that I've gotten hold of the recipe for *fondue*—only it's in French—so we have a translation job ahead of us. . . .

Written at Brest, France
August 2, 1954

Dear Mother and Dadden:

. . . Here's the good word: We're going to Treboul on the coast of Brittany—on the bay of Dournenez, for 2 or 3 days—probably leave on Saturday for Tours. . . . We've had a chance to see a good deal of French rural life that we never expected to see, and in a *way*, we never expected to see it. You should have seen our "hotel" last night—it was really living! . . .

Tours, France
August 8, 1954

Dear Mother and Dadden:

. . . Brittany. . . . Very picturesque—wooden shoes—small coastal villages, and fishing boats built today along the same lines as during the middle ages (except for the addition of diesel engines). We had a chance to look over one of these boats and talk to some of the crew. They fish for tuna, eels and rays—and they stay at sea for about 25 days at a stretch. . . .

By the way, I got your letters, Mother—both of them—with the money. They hit the spot right where the doctor ordered, too, believe me. It may seem as if I've been spending a lot of money, but in Geneva it took $40 for those two clocks—and then the food was so scanty at the Maison that we found ourselves eating quite a bit outside on our own. Switzerland was *not* a cheap country to live in. . . .

Thanks, folks, for coming through in the clutch. . . . See you soon.

Circle Concordia
41 Rue Tournefort
Paris, (Sein) France
August 16, 1954

Dear Mother and Dadden:

It is now Monday night, our last day on the continent. . . . Tomorrow we take the boat train to Cherbourg where we'll catch the "Neptunia." I'm sorry to leave Paris . . . but, it's going to be mighty good to see "Liberty" again in N.Y. harbor. . . .

Once, wandering alone about Geneva, enjoying the town and the lake, time passed unheeded. On returning to his pension Ben found himself locked out. He stretched out at a nearby park and went to sleep. Sometime in the night he was wakened by an elderly man bending over him. In his American French, Ben said, "Oui, monsieur! Qu'est-ce que c'est? Que desirez-vous?" Reporting the incident, Ben laughed, "I think it was my terrible French that frightened him away." He slept on until wakened by the sunrise.

In the visit to the Brittany coast, he wandered on and on over precarious rocks and escarpments until he was about two miles away from his group—seeking the most advantageous camera shot. The beautiful pictures he brought back indicated the treacherous rock path pointing into the sea where he stood to film the coast.

Later, seeing the pictures, his mother exclaimed, "Didn't it occur to you that had anything happened, none of your companions would have known where you were?"

"Mother, in that gorgeous spot nobody could think of companions or be afraid. The view was so overpowering, and being there alone, drinking in the depth of that beauty—was so perfect. What I saw and felt there was the big moment of the whole trip. I prize this picture more than any. The Matterhorn is a close second."

CHAPTER 3

Amherst—Sophomore Year

BEN WONDERED about joining a fraternity. Would there be social snobbishness? His father counselled, "Do what you think is right and best. Look at the members and ask, Do I want them as my close friends? I imagine if all the rituals were tossed in a basket, you couldn't tell one fraternity from another."

Ben was one of a group of about twelve who decided on Chi Psi when invited to pledge. Several of these men were to be a positive force in the fraternity.

Following his death, the president of the fraternity wrote:

> . . . His warmth and sincerity, and particularly his sense of purpose made him one whose company was always sought. His realistic idealism was an excellent influence on all. His fraternity brothers suffered a great loss. I am sure the church has been deprived of one of its greatest future leaders.

Ben took most of the menial "pledge" duties with good grace. Shortly before actual initiation, he was required to write his concept of the fraternity:

> To me a fraternity is two things: First, a fellowship—an organization bound together by friendship; second, it is part of college life. The Lodge should take upon itself the responsibility of maintaining a satisfactory scholastic average, for this is the main function of the college life of which Alpha Chi [Chapter] is a part. The Lodge ought to follow a policy of being a part of Amherst—it should *not* try to isolate itself from the student body or the administration.

After initiation, and seeing the "rushing" from the other side of the fence, he had misgivings. These he expressed in letters to his parents:

Amherst, November 17, 1954

Dear Mother and Dadden:

. . . It sure feels good not to have to cowtow to a lot of rules
and regulations. . . . I was in charge of our Pledge Project—
which consisted of re-modeling a room—making it into a sort of
pantry, to be used during house parties, etc. Can you imagine me
planning and making cabinets, laying a floor, plastering and
painting? I was lost. . . . If it hadn't been for Frank and Pete
who knew something about carpentry, I don't know how we would
ever have finished the thing.

Initiation was quite something. We started out by cleaning out
the yard and putting things in shape around the house. [A de-
tailed account of initiation procedures follows.] . . .

All Friday, from the time we got up 'til we went to bed, we were
supposed to wear full-dress tuxedoes. But since I didn't have one
(it didn't come 'til Saturday), I had a good excuse and wore my
suit. We also couldn't, or weren't supposed to, say a word to anyone the whole day. . . . At any rate, you see that it was quite a
strain keeping up with all of this, plus getting some work done,
plus singing three times over this last Williams weekend. Right
now I'm pretty well shot. . . .

Amherst, February 19, 1955

Dear Mother and Dadden:

Last year, not being "in the know" about how the rushing system worked, I couldn't form any fair opinions. But now I'm able
to see a little better how the thing shapes up, and I'm not sure I
see the point or worth of it all. When you get right down to it,
there's only one function a fraternity serves on a campus such as
Amherst—and that is social.

The fraternity house is the center of relatively all social activity, without it there is no place to go on a date that is convenient.
It's true that you build up some fine friendships and the system
gives you a chance to choose your close friends. But I don't see
that the rushing system (as practiced) is necessary to do these
things.

As far as I can see, the fear, worry, disappointment, and bitter-
ness which rushing invites outbalances the satisfaction and relief
felt by those who make the house of their choice. Rushing forces
those within the fraternity to make judgments on those in the
freshman class. . . . You are saying in effect, "Since you are not
like me, since I do not like you, I will not live with you." As you
say this you are setting yourself up as better than this other per-

son. But the real clincher is that you end up by letting the fellow know you don't have much use for him, and this is no way to get along with people. It doesn't seem fair, or in any way justified. . . .

The Glee Club concert is this next Monday (at Smith). Then we embark for Washington on Tuesday for a Constitution Hall performance and back again Thursday morning.

His boundless interest in and affection for people—particularly those of his own age, boys and girls alike—is reflected in correspondence at this time with a young lady from Sweden whom he had met on the trip to Europe in 1954. There was an emotional attachment between her and one of Ben's pals. But the relationship was troubling to the young lady. She shared her questions and hurts with her friend, Ben, who responded liberally with his thought and counsel.

Dear _____:

. . . Love offers us all the goodness and happiness in the world, but at the same time, it demands faith, and it requires a lot too in worry and fear, and sometimes even tragedy. This is not to say that these things are the "bad" side of love—that we ought to dread them. I think that it's these very things which make love mean so much to a person. Through these things you can find a depth of understanding for what is *truly* worthwhile such as you would not get if you were *always* content, and sure of yourself. Love is a *humbling* experience—it makes you forget "self" and place all your interests, hopes, fears, all your ideals and dreams into common lot with those of the person you love. It it when two people do this that they become "one" in their understanding and purpose. To me, this is what we mean when we say two people are in love. . . .

Amherst, March 24, 1955

Dear _____:

. . . This is a good time of the year for me. In the first place, it's been a beautiful day and I feel spring is not far away. I have been living for this day for weeks. . . . I get so tired of winter, and yearn to see a patch of green grass. I must admit, though, that for me this summer won't compare with last summer's glory. I'm going to be working in a gas station, not too much that's "glorious" in that. But after all, there's money to be made, and the work will do me a lot of good. . . .

Amherst, September 17, 1955

Dear _____:

. . . When I started this letter, I was going to make it simple,
light and chatty. But I must say what is in my mind. We are
good friends, and we have always seemed to have a good understanding of one another. There is no other way for two such persons to talk to one another *except* openly and frankly. . . .

On the day you sailed I noticed a heaviness of spirit which was
more than just a "too short vacation; lots of work ahead" feeling.
This seemed so real to me that I became heavy-hearted too. As we
waited for the ship to pull out, standing on the dock looking
across at each other—H. and I at you, and you at us—talking
and laughing now and again; and as the *Stockholm* finally slipped
out into the river, I kept thinking, "You are trying not to show
that you are sad, but you are."

I didn't understand your sadness and I still don't. Whatever
may have been troubling you inside, don't brood over the past—
look ahead always; keep your head high; find your ideal, and keep
your eyes on it. Live and work in the spirit of this that you believe in, in spite of yourself. You are a rare and refreshing sort of
person, spontaneous and sincere in your relationships with other
people—without ulterior motives (or at least just a little now and
then). This is what makes you "yourself" and so thoroughly lik-
able.

I hope you will forgive me, if have offended you in any of this.
That was not my intention. I write only in the spirit of the talks
we had together this summer. And I hope you will know, too,
that I am forever your friend,

Ben.

To his Christmas card Ben added a personal note:

"CHRISTMAS—with a magic that no other time can bring,
A wondrous glory that lights the earth and makes the whole world
sing.

CHRISTMAS—with a happiness that makes it stand apart.
CHRISTMAS—may its many joys and treasures fill your heart."

*   *   *

Bronxville, New York
December 1955

Dear _____:

This is just to say "Hello! how are you?" at a wonderful time
of the year.

Though it's vacation, there's little time to relax. I have a great deal of school work before I go back and it is going to be pretty hard to get everything done while "frolicking" (know the word?— means "having a lot of fun") on the white sands of *Bermuda!* The Double Quartet has been asked to be a part of a college variety show under the auspices of the Defense Department to entertain our troops, etc. All expenses paid for a week. Needless to say, we were very happy to oblige. I'm only sorry that I won't be able to be here at home as long as I would like. Christmas is a time to be with one's family. . . .

I hope your outlook is still as positive and happy as it sounded in your last letter (to which this is a poor excuse as an answer!).

Regards to your parents—and Merry, Merry Christmas!

Your friend,
Ben.

Amherst, February 19, 1956

Dear _____ :

Thanks for your letter. It really gives a person a lift to receive news from a good friend who is "far away across the sea." Today I caught myself humming the "Lucky Strike" tune, and it made me think of a certain day in New York City, with two people stumbling along the streets loaded down with packages—and you kept singing this song. . . .

I'm so glad to hear you will be in Paris this summer, and I look forward to meeting your boy friend, who, I'm sure, must be quite a wonderful fellow.

Traveling to a foreign country is just about worthless if you can't make personal contact with individuals in that country. . . . You have a pretty good understanding of the American and "what makes him tick" (as we say); because you lived with us for a time and saw *how* we do things and *why*. You learned our attitudes as you have heard us express them in specific situations. This sort of understanding has a lot more meaning than that surrounding such phrases as "les riches Americans" or "energetic Scandinavia."

Tell B. that in catching you he has caught himself a very special sort of girl.

Write again and so long for now.

Bronxville, September 5, 1956

Dear _____ :

I landed in New York on Saturday, September 1st, and you can imagine my delight when I opened your letter and realized that possibly you were at the altar at the very minute I was reading of all the joy and promise which your words seemed to hold. How glad I was to hear this wonderful news, for I have always felt you were a girl who needed very much to find someone to whom you could give yourself completely and in perfect trust; and you have been selfish only in your strong desire to find this outlet for the energy of your heart and soul. . . . The first time I met you on that excursion in the hills around Lausanne, I was struck by the way you could make people smile and laugh and enjoy the moment in which they found themselves. Then, as I came to know you better, I was struck even more by your sensitive awareness of the different qualities of experience.

Your thought runs deep, your personality has broad dimensions—perceptive, but a great zest for living, a passionate energy, and a strong belief in the joy and goodness of life.

I am expressing these things only to let you know how and in what way I am happy for you. This is the way it ought to be between friends. I think that at the core of your being you have cherished a faith in the joy to be realized as two people give themselves to each other in love and trust. Because of this you felt so keenly the hurt of your experience with H—, here you saw this faith betrayed—its trust denied. But then, as so often happens, when you felt lost you found yourself and all that you had believed in this man who is now your husband. What a wealth of meaning this word, "husband," and its counterpart "wife," must have for you.

Through the meaning with which you surround these words, as you live with and for each other, you can look out on the world about you and know that there is a pervasive joy running through all experience. Even through grief and sorrow and loneliness and despair, we can cherish this faith—and especially you and your husband, for in finding each other, you have found and know the truth of this faith.

> Your friend,
> Ben.

Hans, an exchange student from Zurich, Switzerland, had become a friend of the Symon family while visiting in their home. This Christmas letter of 1954 typifies the warmth and capacity for sharing that marked Ben's association with countless young people.

Dear Hans,

This is just a note to thank you for your most generous gift. You have no idea how good that cheese is going to taste at school, when at about midnight I feel like taking a break and having a little snack before hitting the sack. I am a great lover of cheese, and I certainly appreciate this which you have sent.

About that book you wanted of Dr. Peale's. I sent that one and another, by Dr. Ditzen, quite some time ago . . . I'm sorry, Hans, I wanted them to reach you for Christmas.

I hope you had a happy holiday with your family and that you are all well and in good spirits. Christmas should, I think, leave us with a deep feeling of satisfaction, and an awareness of the best which we know in us. . . .

I am staying close to home this next summer to earn some money. . . . My ideal would be to get over for a long enough time to learn French well, so that I may feel some sort of command of the language. At the moment, however, this is no more than an idle dream. . . .

Best of luck, Hans, in the year ahead, and pass along my regards to your parents for me.

Your friend,
Goodie

A few months later Ben describes the preparation which would take him more fully into literary and philosophical channels:

Amherst, May 22, 1955

Dear Mother and Dadden,

Just realized as I wrote the date that today is Bob's birthday. If you should talk to him in the next couple of days or so, tell him "Happy Birthday" for me.

Next year I'm business manager of the Double Quartet, which means keeping track of finances and correspondence . . . two categories of activity in which I shine with brilliant mediocrity. . . .

I have provisionally signed my fate as an English major for the next two years. . . . I think that in examining literature you find the most accurate and full expression of the temperaments and emotions of people within the context of the period in which they lived. To me this is important—because what a person thinks or feels and what he does . . . this is what that person "is." This is not expressed well, but it seems to me that literature, if it's good, may express something of the ways in which the common motivations and hopes and fears of men are worked out in individual experience. Good literature is a testimony of some phase of human experience; this is why it appeals to people from generation to generation, and why it is valuable. . . .

The way my schedule stands right now for next year, I'll be

taking 3 English courses in each semester, a psychology course, a
philosophy course, and a couple of French literature courses. It's
going to be heavy going because all of these will load me up with
a tremendous amount of reading. This, plus DQ, Glee Club,
Chapel Choir, plus Sphinx, is going to leave little time to catch
my breath. I'll have to get a little work done this summer, especially in French. Sounds good on paper, but I wonder how much
I'll actually accomplish. . . .

Also during this second year, Ben prepared, for a course in
religion, a paper titled, "Christianity: My Understanding of It
and My Relationship to It." The closing section, "My Unresolved
Predicament," is indicative of his personal thought and involve-
ment:

I am a child of my time and have been nurtured in the Protestant tradition, but, nevertheless, it seems to me that modern
Protestant thinking has come closest to expressing the essentials
of Christianity. Christianity still may be reduced to the simple
act of giving up oneself in Christ. Christianity is God the Father,
God the Son, and God the Holy Spirit. It is not man finding
God; it is God, in his grace, finding man and confronting him
with the gift of His love and redemption in Jesus Christ. Christianity is man's free choice to believe in God's love (which is in
Christ) in spite of himself and his doubt. Moreover, it is an active
commitment which commands all of man in every sphere of his
activity. This, it seems to me, is the recurrent, dominant theme of
Christianity. It is the commitment of man to God, transcendent,
but uniquely revealed in the man, Jesus Christ.

I have felt the impact of the words of Christ: "Ye have not
chosen me; but I have chosen you." And I know, in my own mind
and heart, that one day I am going to have to answer this call or
forfeit my desire for meaning in life. Still I hesitate. I am not
looking for some sudden revelation in my life. I realize that insight may come slowly and grow to the moment of decision. This
is my unresolved predicament: knowledge of and desire for the
call of Christianity, but no personal experience of it in my life.

A number of young people spoke to Mr. and Mrs. Symon of
the impact of Ben's conviction. One said, "I so envied Ben's faith."
Another, "Ben was far ahead of the rest of us. He found the
answers that most of us are still yearning for. The Beatnik stuff—
what we hear on TV, together with what the writers throw at us
—along with other philosophy that is empty and despairing—
doesn't help us find the answers."

With Ben's studies in literature came an interest in poetry. His own attempts to write it were varied, sometimes touched with humor, as when registering an aversion to time schedules:

I think a clock a strange and joyless thing,
Since it rules us if we will or no.
I'd wish that I were free to laugh and sing,
That time would let me hear the breezes blow,
Except I know for sure that I may not:
For I have many pressing tasks to do,
By express command of milord, the clock,
Who's sure to see that I am never through.
Then who's there says that we are truly free
Or that in time a man may ever flee
The hours and the minutes; for they combine
To make me sit and think and write these lines,
And I am sure, as sure as I can be,
That I would rather go and climb a tree.

He became intent on experimenting with the techniques and styles of the masters, such as this, called "Prince Louis Orsini (An Episode in Padova)" which followed Browning:

My rank is high, be careful what you say—
The charge you bear is grave—(nay, stay my men)—
What's this! Her bloody fate you speak to me
And dare to stain my name with such filth and shame?
I stand wronged!—(now clap your swords my men, say yea)
You call yourselves the Corte, but what pray tell
Have you now to do? Give me peace I say! The world
Is wide and dark and deep, and shelters men
Whose hearts burn black within—Yea, black, as thine
If truth be known—(now men, stand close on guard)—
Then know my own inquiry's just begun,
And all within good time will come to light. . . .
Well, yes 'tis true we quar'lled—but with cause I say!—
For all her husband's means she kept from me.
He dead, to me his brother should have left
A goodly share, for we in blood were linked.
You've called me rudely hence to plead my case,
And thus I have fulfilled your law—
(Hear my men, for they will bear me out)—
Keep silence then, and open not your mouths,
For know my rank is high and all my men stand nigh.

The second year at Amherst ended with Ben's summary: "It's simply wonderful. I am more interested than ever in what I am doing and studying."

He worked that summer for the Shell Oil Company, which had assigned him to survey a sizeable number of filling stations in the New York area and ascertain the cost of painting them as a check against estimates already submitted. Ben made inquiries as to how to do the job and followed the counsel. He completed the survey and estimates, doublechecked, and wrote up his evaluation.

His boss was impressed with the report and reproduced copies of it as a model. The experience ended with Ben happy to have made money toward a European trip, but also confident that he didn't want to spend his life in business. The dimensions of commerce and industry were not deep enough to capture him fully. He must look in other directions for his life work.

CHAPTER 4
Amherst—Junior Year

LETTERS TO his parents gave proof that all his time was not given over to mysticism, aesthetics, or philosophy:

Amherst, September 20, 1955

Dear Mother and Dadden,—

Our "suite" of rooms has shaped up well. We have three rooms and a bath with tub and shower for four of us. A couple of us rigged up a little study in the attic. We built a flimsy framework out of odds and ends of board from the basement, and then enclosed an area (about 12' by 7') with cardboard, using the framework to keep the whole thing standing. We are going to invest in a couple of cheap electric heaters to see us through the winter. . . . All for the sake of study. . . . Rather noble of us, don't you think?

Yesterday we made an addition—a small refrigerator. It was only $40 ($10 apiece). It will be a two-year investment and will enhance the selling value of the room when we move out.

Amherst, February 12, 1956

Dear Mother and Dadden,—

We went on a clean-up binge today in preparation for rushing which starts next week. This is a time I really dread. What we have is a preoccupation with the "cult of the Collegiate gentleman." Rushing is the evil; not fraternity living.

Of an anticipated European trip he wrote:

I am eager to learn French and get to know the Frenchman—to anticipate his smile, his frown, his word of interest or indifference, his fear and concern. I want to have a sense of the values and motivations of the person.

To a friend, Ben vividly reports his reaction to Homecoming at Amherst.

Amherst, October 23, 1955

Dear N____

What a crowd! So many people, and most of them making complete fools of themselves. I was sitting in "the Great Hall" just sort of running through the first movement of the "Moonlight," when a woman in her late 40s came over and flopped on the piano bench beside me. . . . She had a cigarette angling out of her mouth, a glazed look in her eyes. She sat down *very* close to me and said, "This is really awfully nice, and I just love classical. Why don't you play some bad music and wake up all these stupid people? Don't you ever smile?—(at this point I guess I wasn't smiling)—Don't you like to play? How about a 'teensy' one? Why don't you play some bad music?," and on and on—She was just one of many.

I said, "Do you have to smile to enjoy playing?" She said, "I guess I'm not very smart about these things." And I said, "Well, you know, you really shouldn't admit that," etc., etc.

I'm just glad this week-end comes only once a year. I don't think I'll be able to bring myself back as an alumnus. At one of these affairs you're watching an "exposition" of slow degeneration —and it is all so completely useless.

Then this morning Peter and I went to Church and heard a sermon on "loving those we don't like." It was a general description of Christian love—it was so great! It said the things I've been trying to clarify in my own mind. Christian love is not sentiment—not "moon, noon, swoon"; it is beyond personal likes and dislikes. (This is the "going out beyond oneself" idea.) It is a question of "the will of God"—"Not my will, but Thine"—Action in spite of me. This is the ideal of the love of Christ, who loved with a compassion so great that He could humble Himself and die *for sin*—for all that is bad: hate, fear, pride, and all the rest— and yet gain a victory in his love which said, "Forgive them. . . ." As Thayer Green put it, the humility of Christ was "terrifying and overwhelming."

I'm being convinced more and more of the reality and "validness" of the Christian commitment. There is nothing so basic as this concept of love which can link us to a power beyond our own. We see people every day who are examples of the inadequacy of our own wills in running our lives (like that woman . . . an extreme, I admit).

In Ben's second European trip, one of his traveling companions reported it was more important to Ben to chat with a French farmer than to reach a planned destination on time. Works of art could hold him, oblivious to the passing minutes, as he sought for their message about the times that produced them. He said, "Their dedication and perfection glorifies God and the adoration of the divine in life. I find them a challenge to our modern world."

A notebook shows his gusty appreciation, as well as a sharpened discrimination:

On Shipboard
June 8, 1956

It is a new sort of world when you are in it alone, even for as short a time as a single day. In a dialogue between two persons, we are aware of gestures and words, gauging our responses by what we feel to be their "mood." But in aloneness one comes to know the tenor of his own feelings. This is a kind of withdrawal that has a value all its own.

There is power, which I feel buoying me up in a world turned into a "brilliant, shimmering awareness of the qualities of a momentary impression and in its sense of movement from one such moment through another." This is what I was thinking as I lolled in my deck chair, and the stimulus was Virginia Woolf's essay on Chaucer's capacity as a poet. . . .

"It is certainly a fine day."

I had to break off and turn to the man who eased into the chair beside me. "Yes, it really couldn't be better," I answered.

He was an Irish priest—Father Coyle of Londonderry and Birmingham. We talked of England and America, the place of tradition, Eastern culture.

But the transition between Virginia Woolf, the rhythm of poetry, and the impression of an Irish priest in transit between America and England was a sharp one, and emphasized the disparity between social and private communication.

June 9, 1956. My table companions are three. Mrs. Pflanza, an elderly lady from Tennessee, a teacher of German extraction, going to visit her son and his German wife in München. The others, Mrs. Geissler and her daughter, Ingrid, are German born, returning to Stuttgart for a visit after living in the U.S. since 1952.

Mrs. Geissler recalled her experiences during the war years when she lived in Stuttgart. "Ingrid was only five years when it started. She never had to march in the youth groups and she never really knew what it was in those times."

Mrs. Pflanza broke in, "We forget so quickly. My daughter-in-law had to work on a farm—forced labor—very little food. The owner was a Nazi who became angry if he saw his wife make the sign of the cross at a meal." So it went: hard times, fear, and death imminent in every moment. . . .

Yet, after twenty minutes of this, Mrs. Geissler was smiling. "I think there are more good people than bad in the world." She spoke slowly, with a quiet assurance issuing from depths . . . "and even in the bad, if you look hard enough, you can find some good." No one could deny her vision of life redeeming itself from generation to generation.

June 10, 1956. Tonight an interesting man sat down at our table. He was Dutch, tall, and a little awkward in our group. There are depths in his eyes and spontaneity in his smile. His speech is simple and direct, even as his faith. He commands a respect, as for something solid and durable—a granite knoll in the morning sunlight.

Aix—Cézanne Exposition—Portraits (those techniques)—
1.—"La Maison sur La Marne"—lake, trees, chateau . . . shady greens in reflected water. "Le Foret"—light sparkling through leaves of light green.
2. "Cemetierre"—lonely tombstone resting almost hidden and forgotten in the shadows behind a wall. Light shimmers outside the shadows . . . effect, "light and shadows" or "life and death."

July 31, 1956. All well. God, be with us, for we are yet humble and uncertain in the world. Oh, how fortunate we are! I pray that we may profit from these days. Happy anniversary Mother! [Mrs. Symon received red roses from Ben that day.]

Piacenza—"Duomo"—Seeing it in the evening. Dim, cool—a grand scene of mystery . . . stout, straight columns stretching into the dim unknown above in the dark heights of nave and cupola. What a place to pass a few moments of silence! The moment is swallowed in Eternity.

Padua—"St. Anthony Basilica"—Something delicate and intricate is realized in a grand design. The faithful whisper and do homage —the marble facing worn and smoothed by many hands. One caress and the heart is lightened. . . .

Venice—the brilliance and mystery of the East is mingled with Renaissance genius. Step into a gondola. Lights shining across water, distant music. Palaces lit softly, by watery aquas and greens, line the canals with a delicate mysterious lacework of colonnades and arches. "Romantic" does not encompass the quality of this hour!

Piazzo San Marco—is the crossroads for all tourist traffic passing north or south between Italy and France and the German speaking countries. One can sense the eagerness in every group, for in Venice one expects to taste enjoyment in each moment.

August 15, 1956. I find myself high up (about 1700m.—4000ft.) in the Simplon Pass. As I bumped up the steep slopes in second gear and then braked onto the long down coast, the falling sun left blue depths in treacherous gorges and delicate rose tints in the towering peaks. There was magic in the vast dimensions. At the Hotel Belle-Vue a gay throng of German-Swiss folk were gathered on a terrace. I was tempted to ask the price of meal and bed for the night; but, being a good Scot, I felt the wisest course was to get on.

A little further down the slope I came upon another much smaller auberge. The sound of an accordion and the snug look of the place made me stop. It was only 4.50 for the room and 4 for the dinner (around $2.50 in all). Having gone this far, I was in the mood of extravagance. Besides, the mountain air made me shiver and think of a cozy bed.

The girl who helped around the place led me to the back and up a narrow flight of stairs to my room. She had straw-colored hair, rosy cheeks, a fresh, crisp apron. Just the sort of person you would expect to go along with the setting. I never slept in a more comfortable bed—soft and deep, piled high with quilts and a feathery comforter, it all but filled the tiny pine-paneled room. There was no light, only a small candle next to the bed with a package of matches placed close by. Plumbing was lacking, a pitcher and basin substituting.

The next morning was beautiful! Sun, sky, peaks, hills and valleys—all sparkling in the fresh morning air! Having enjoyed both this and the softer hues of the evening before, I was about as content as I have ever been before or since. Deciding to spend the night as I did, was probably one of the better ideas I have had.

August 16, 1956. Evening at Nyon—auberge. Dinner—bread, cheese, apples, plums, chocolate—sitting on a wall next to the lake dangling my feet over the lapping water below. The lake was taking on a silvery blue glow in the evening twilight. Mont Blanc rose in the distance, its snow-covered caps (one can actually distinguish four) reflected the last rays of the sun. In the foreground, a swan, drifting soundlessly and aimlessly, hardly visible in the misty evening air. . . . There were people about on either side of me, encamping along the bank. Their laughter and chatter—as they finished their evening meal and prepared for the night, left a sense of private contentment in tune with the surroundings.

Next morning I lathered up, hurried to my scooter where I shaved before my rear-view mirror—the only glass I could find in the whole place. Then back upstairs to pack. But first I enjoyed a long look out the window overlooking the lake. The water had the same silver glow it had had the evening before. Some stratified clouds stretched carelessly along the horizon. There was no trace of Mont Blanc, hidden in the morning mist. But you knew it was there. Below me on the gravel terrace, a man was sitting at a table with an open book. I thought "Well, sir, you strike a fine pose— From all appearances you are using profitably these early morning hours. I wonder what you are reading? Is it philosophy, politics, literature? Where lies your interest?"

A traveling companion for a time wrote later to Mrs. Symon:

Ben and I saw a lot of each other during our summer in France. I have never had a finer friend. He was so intensely interested in others—all others. Time and again in France Ben was going out of his way to make friends. He was absorbing the land and its people far more deeply than I ever could.

Letters and postcards to parents and friends tell how he responded not alone to the monumental creations of man, but to human beings and the natural world:

Florence, June 21, 1956

Dear Mother and Dadden,—

I am sitting now in the parlor or "salon" of this pension; and since it is just after dinner, almost all the exam-burdened students are sitting in little groups, smoking or talking. This is a sort of informal "come-together." It seems to form after every meal—a moment of relaxation. It's odd to be on the outside of this, looking in. I can't understand a word of what they're saying, and to them I am some strange creature to whom they can only turn a curious glance now and then.

This is unfortunate for if we cannot speak to each other, how can we communicate—even be *polite* with each other. How important communication is! When you cannot talk to anyone else, you become aware of the world of words within yourself and this inner conversation becomes very important. You have time to make a thought complete.

Wherever you turn, there is something to see—and it is always either delightful or over-powering. The former describes the city itself—sunny—full of light and color, the people full of a natural exuberance. The heritage of the city is what is overpowering— the tangible glory of the greatest period of artistic expression in the history of western culture. It doesn't make any difference whether I can speak Italian or not for a visit as short as this. There is enough here for anyone to enjoy and profit from even if he were both deaf and dumb.

Love,
Goodie

Milan, June 26, 1956

Here, for two nights, I'm paying 50¢. Not living in luxury, but I have a bed (dormitory style) on which I spread out my sleeping bag. There's a cold shower which, though painful, serves the purpose. Also, Dadden, you may be interested to know that I've learned to shave with cold water—it really isn't so bad.

Paris, July 4, 1956

Just pulled into Paris last night. It was really quite a trip—not as long as I had expected—only about 700 miles. Lambretta works very well.

Paris, July 11, 1956

Steve and I have a fine room, complete with parquet floors, French windows, grilled balcony, plus breakfast in the room every morning at 8:15, "a la mode francaise."

I can eat lunch in town for less than 100 frs. ($.28). When we did this, our landlady cut down her price to 1600 frs.

Every day I meet someone new at the dinner table. None seems to show any real interest in the fact that we are here. I know most of the people here only as "Madame" or "Monsieur." The French, as individuals, are reserved. The family circle is a very closely knit unit.

Their intimacy must either be buried so deep under tradition and formality that, to the outsider, it hardly seems existent; or it is devoid of the glow of personal affection—I don't know which. I

would guess the first. But after I've written all this, I think about
the Roos family. With them there was such a warmth of hospi-
tality. I suppose it boils down to this—with them I was a guest,
and here I'm a boarder. If this is the difference then what a world
of difference there is!

When we tell anyone around here we took the weekend in
Champagne, they say "Mais, ce province, ce n'est pas interessant."
But for us it was wonderful. Imagine a perfect summer day, brilliant coloring of cultivated fields, ripening wheat, rich green
topping of corn and sugar beets mingling with the more pastel
shadow of vineyards stretching away into the distance. There are
hills, but they are long, easy slopes rolling out like a ruffled
carpet. The sky is an innocent blue. The clouds are small and
delicate, like little puffs of cotton. The sun is hot. But there is
always a shady place where you can lean against a tree, and, in
perfect contentment, pull out your bread, cheese and wine. It
makes a fine moment to remember.

Verdun. We saw the famous forts where the French held off
the Germans (notably Forte de Vauz et Forte de Slouaumont). A
plaque in memory of the last pigeon which the Commandant
(Captaine Ramoney, I think) sent out for help. The pigeon arrived safely—half dead from inhaling the gas in the air. The
French have immortalized it, along with Ramoney's last words
to the outside world: "C'est mon dernier pigeon."

Mont St. Michel retains a kind of cold simplicity in its vertical
lines which makes you recall the aesthetic devotion of the
cloistered monks of medievel times. This is evident in the interior
where thin rounded columns cluster together and reach toward
the ceiling where they bend gracefully into a restful (but struc-
turally complex) pattern of rounded arches and vaults. This
rounded arch requires a great deal of support, and to offset this
kind of aesthetic preoccupation or yearning for the celestial world
beyond this "vale of tears," you have the stolid bulk of heavy
pillars (some weighing as much as eight tons) girding up the
delicate vaults. *You feel as if here is an expression of man's age-old
attempt to link the imminent "here and now" with that field of
life and action which he feels must exist beyond the tangible con-
fines of his own finite knowledge.* Here is a truly noble effort.

Sirmione, August 14, 1956

Dear Mother and Dadden:

All is going well. If you have a map handy, you can follow our
route down south of Milano to Pavia where, just outside the
town, we came to the "Certosa di Pavia"—a Carthaginian Monas-

tery started in 1396 and built through the 15-16th centuries. Light fell softly into every chapel and corner of the three great naves. There was a cool, luminous beauty which was at once humbling and refreshing.

From Pavia on to Piacenza where, in the dim light of evening, the huge nave and crowning cupolas, flickering candles and a penetrating silence, seemed to swallow you up in eternity.

From here to Parma where we spent the night "en camping." The next morning, we spent time in Parma (art gallery and another "Duomo"—interior completely covered with frescoes). Then we scooted up to Mantua where we were guided (we never could have found our own way) through the Ducal Palace—one of the largest in the world, covering three km. I can imagine it more grand than Versailles. There are hanging gardens looking off the great dining room 2 stories up—frescoes, relief work, marble— and rooms seeming to stretch around without end. (Throughout the week, the weather was perfect—hot sun, blue sky and cool shadows. We ate a lot of Italian ice cream, "Gelati," the best I ever put in my mouth.)

We spent the night in Verona in a cheap hotel. There was only one bed, so Bob blew up the air mattress to his sleeping bag and slept on the brick floor—one of the dirtiest I've seen anywhere. I had the bed, but it really wasn't much better. I slept in a sort of "U-shape. . . ."

Finally, Vicenza, Padua (where we saw St. Antony's Basilica. This, next to the Certosa, was the high for me as far as churches were concerned. Even San Marco in Venice was not to outdo this one for its beauty and majesty), and Venice, the end of the line.

We left our scooters outside the city and caught the ferry heading down the Grand Canal. It was after dark, but even then Venice was very much alive.

There is more to tell—a gondola ride in the evening with two *very* charming South African girls (O, la! la! as the French say), and then all the time we spent wandering here and there—and all the art (one gallery with 50 paintings of Tintoretto). I am really glad I went. Now I am on my way back to Geneva. I am in a small resort town on Lake Garda this afternoon and plan to go back into Verona tonight to hear Tosca in the Arena.

Love,
Goodie

P.S. Has Grandmother come yet? If so, say hello and say I'm sorry I've been so remiss with my letter writing.

LeHavre, August 22, 1956

Dear Mother and Dadden:

Traveling by scooter has allowed me to snoop about outside the usual tourist lanes, and this experience I'll never forget. But when all's said and done, I'm going to be mighty glad to set feet on home ground. Clear the decks for *four square meals* a day! Junior's hungry!

Love,
Goodie

This summer made a glorious experience in preparing for the final year of college.

His poem after "In Memoriam," bespeaks what was growing in Benjamin Goodall Symon:

> The hills afar now show to men
>   The truth of Ages long since past;
>   How streams in Time run swift and fast,
> And all in all is Change—But then
>
> A wind sighs softly in the trees,
>   And whispers me the Truth which I
>   Have known and felt, yet know not why;
> And soul breathes "Yea," and all is peace.

Increasingly, he was saying "Yea" to the truths that speak to the spirit and which give a steadying anchor beneath the waves and tides of the surface.

CHAPTER 5

Amherst—Senior Year

Conformity is going to destroy the moral fiber of our country and cause our downfall. My generation must wake up to its weakness." This feeling of Ben's probably prompted his ventures in the aesthetic fields as described in the *Student,* Amherst's undergraduate publication:

> Benjamin G. Symon, Jr., a senior, is vice-chairman of the recently organized Fine Arts Committee, which plans to present a series of dramatic, musical, and artistic programs to point up relationships between religion and the arts. The student body will be asked to consider the nature of religious experience as related to creative modes of expression in drama, music and painting.

Ben and George Moses spent several days visiting art galleries in New York City to select pictures for the planned exhibit. As a result of their study, twenty oils, nineteen etchings of Rouault's *Miserere,* and other selected pieces led to an exhibit of significance to the campus and community.

Later in the school year, the *Student* carried this item:

> A new [Christian Association] committee has been formed to investigate the role of religion. Discussion meetings, in which members of the faculty, students of various faiths, and outside speakers will be invited to participate, will be important sources of information. The treatment of religion in the present curriculum will be studied by Benjamin Symon '57. Interactions of the Department of Religion with other departments will be discussed.

Some selections from a paper, "Man Divided and Man Against God," reflect Ben's understanding:

> With Jesus, the issues are very clear: It is man against himself and against God. Man is divided on the one hand by his consum-

41

ing desire to believe in something "better" beyond himself, and on the other hand, by the frustrating presence of his doubt and disbelief. He is haunted by the shadow of uncertainty hanging over him, and by his ego, which cannot bear to give up the sense of its own importance. With the coming of Jesus, the choice allows for no misunderstanding: "Whom say ye that I am?" says Jesus. The choice literally stands before us, and we hear the challenging words of Elijah echoing down from the Old Testament: "If God be God, follow him; but if Baal be God, then follow him!"

It seems perfectly simple. All we have to do is make up our minds to believe in Jesus as the only begotten Son of the Father, and we may take our place in the ranks of the Blessed. If only it were so easy. But man is divided against himself. Even as he confesses his willingness to serve God, he cherishes in his heart the latent desire to be God himself. It is like the story of the rich young man who approaches Jesus and asks Him what he must do to enter into the Kingdom of Heaven. "Sell all your goods, and follow me," says Jesus. The man is unable to do this and turns away with sorrow in his heart. There is in every man the self that would believe, and the self that will not.

Jesus gives us a way to connect ourselves with our vision of perfection—of "something better" beyond this that we know here and now. The universal has become particular in Him. The "Word" has "become flesh and dwelt among us." God has come to meet us, and in so doing, He has given us the choice to believe in Him—the chance to live, as Kirkegaard's "Knight of Faith," in the infinite and finite at the same time.

This study as well as other lines of intellectual pursuit were spokes for the ever strengthening hub of faith and personal commitment.

Chosen a candidate for a Rotary scholarship for study abroad, Ben stated his purpose:

My primary objective in going abroad to study theology at the University of Edinburgh is to discover and define my relationship to the Christian faith and to consider the Christian ministry as a vocation. I choose Edinburgh because I think there I would most likely gain a good grounding in Calvinistic theology.

I used to look at the minister as a kind of ideal figure, acting in the pleasant and secure role of a man who "knows all the answers." I now see the minister as a man deeply immersed in the complexities of social intercourse and private anxiety, unique only in that he has something to affirm in terms of a traditional and systemic view of experience. . . .

I feel that any decisions I make will be much more certain if I am able to make them against the background of a year's contact with the Christian faith in an environment foreign to that which I had known. . . .

The nations of the world look out upon one another with fear and distrust. The Christian must be on the lookout for ways in which to reach beyond his own limited society to apprehend the meaning of this word "christian" in other countries of the world. As he does, he is much more likely to gain a sense of his own personal commitment within this "community of believers."

Ben's enthusiasm for Christmas was boundless. It was for him the happiest of holidays. The joy of receiving and giving, the songs, the sparkle and color, he summed up: "It's the biggest birthday party in all the world." Each year he wanted a brighter star for the tree, a new set of lights or more decorations, and his camera was always ready for Christmas morning.

Prior to going home for Christmas, Ben had a brief Christmas Service with his roommates at their fraternity house. One reported later, "I still can picture Ben seated on the sofa facing the door as he read so well the Bible story of the Birth of Christ."

His mother described that Christmas of 1956:

Ben's last Christmas was the most complete we can ever know as a family. He and Bob were at home with Bob's lovely wife, Langston, and their baby, Beth! On Christmas Eve we went to the traditional Christmas pageant, held annually on the hillside lawn of the Reformed Church in the center of the village. The clear moonlight and starry sky cast a spell of mystery and the heart felt peace within. All traffic had been halted since five o'clock. Ben, as he had done for years, was high on the hill in the darkness singing with the hidden "angels' voices."

After the pageant we met at the home of friends for supper. Ben's face was aglow. "Did you all feel as I do, that that was the most beautiful pageant we've ever had? Even the donkey behaved himself," he said, laughing. "He didn't balk as usual. Maybe it was that moon, or just me, remembering that I won't be here for all this next year; but it all gripped me with a feeling of reality. Bonnie old Scotland won't have anything to take the place of home for Christmas."

Later in the evening Ben joined his group of young people for their annual caroling. The night after Christmas, Ben, his date and others went through falling snow to carol again. Near midnight they came to our home for hot chocolate. Ben tiptoed upstairs to show off "the most adorable and amazing baby you ever saw!" Later we talked of our happy Christmas together—the joy of having Bob and his family with us, and then of the spirit of Christmas. . . . Ben said, "It's the wonder and the burst of joy and good will that thrills me. The world seems good. If only that spirit would stay!"

With his decision to enter Seminary, it was necessary to gain approval by the "Consistory," made up of Elders and Deacons, in his local Church. On that occasion in February of 1957 when he was asked to tell of his motives in entering Seminary, his remarks were direct and sincere. He wasn't positive he was going to be a minister of the Gospel. "I want to use my life for Christian service and this study is necessary for me to know how and in what field I can serve best." He made it clear he wanted the surest evidence that the ministry was the one calling for him.

The Consistory's recommendation to the Yale Divinity School, which he planned to enter after Edinburgh, and a letter from a member of the Amherst faculty show the esteem in which he was held:

February 17, 1957

The Consistory of this Church at its meeting on February 14, 1957, voted to approve Mr. Benjamin G. Symon, Jr. as a candidate for the ministry. All members of The Consistory who knew Mr. Symon spoke in praise of him. His record here is excellent and we are satisfied with his motivation.

Sincerely yours,
Bronxville Reformed Church
per Hubert A. Howson
Clerk of Consistory

Amherst, March 5, 1957

Dean Liston Pope
New Haven, Connecticut
Dear Liston:

You certainly get the attention of some of our best young men. Benjamin G. Symon, Jr. is one of these. He is a topnotch student, . . . and is in my book an unusually able lad.

Get your hands on him if you can because you'll always congratulate yourself for doing so.

Cordially,
Eugene S. Wilson
Director of Admission

Ben's only boss in the business field was Eugene W. Hennessy of Scarsdale, New York. He had this to say in response to Dean Liston's inquiry:

> Mr. Symon was employed by the Shell Oil Company in the Metropolitan New York area during the summer of 1955. His work was excellent. He knew what was required to do a job thoroughly and expeditiously. He fit well into our organization, being well liked by all people with whom he came in contact. It was immediately apparent to us that he could take an assignment and follow it through without too much supervision; all of which was remarkable for a young man without previous business training.
>
> I can attest to this young man's qualifications for training to aid him in the vocation he is considering.

Ben's capacity for helpful friendship during his college experience is portrayed in a letter from one of his fraternity brothers:

> For two years we did our studying together, huddled up under the Chi Psi roof in the "garrett." I'll never forget one long night together spent thesis writing last spring, each of us busy reading, thinking sporadically and occasionally interrupting the concentration to read aloud for criticism something he had written. Ben used to tell me that what I wrote would sound a lot better if I took out half the words and doubled the number of periods. I can remember many times when I wouldn't have gotten papers in if Ben hadn't pitched in and done part of the typing; once he stayed up with me until 5:00 a.m. What always struck me was not the help he offered unsolicited, but the way he offered it. There was only a single desire to help.
>
> When I got my Marshall scholarship last spring all of my friends were vocal with congratulations, but I don't think any of them was so sincerely excited for me as was Ben.
>
> Ben never took any of his beliefs or feelings for granted; he was not able to let things "just happen." Whether the question at hand involved a girl or his deepest religious convictions, he seemed driven to probe and articulate his "real" feelings and ideas. . . .

But he was always remarkable for his absolute refusal to be cynical. While he was serious and critical, he wasn't afraid of enthusiasm. In moments of depression, it always gave me a boost to be with someone who could say "amazing" and "by ding!," so often.

I think the most exciting visual art experience of our lives we had together in Venice—we stumbled on a Renaissance school decorated entirely with Tintoretto oils. For most of a day we studied the Tintorettos, talking about the remarkable use of light, the captured movement, the vital and even brash, but ingenuously effective treatments of conventional religious subjects. That we knew very little didn't matter very much. Ben had had his glasses stolen the previous night and he was all the more intense with squinting to see more clearly.

Now I'm beginning to ramble—you can see how right was his criticism of too many words and not enough periods.

From a roommate:

Toward the end of the school year, Ben and George double-dated on a Sunday night. I could not join them, as I wanted to finish some assignment. While studying in the next room, I heard them arrive. After saying "Hi" I returned, and no sooner sat back down to study, when I heard Ben mention something on the existence of God. It was different from the usual superficial comments of many college dates. The four of them pored over the subject all evening, presenting and discussing slants which I had never heard or thought of before. I restrained myself as long as possible, and then joined in the discussion. Goodie mixed some humor, incidents of faith, and profound ideas, and his companions were equally as diverse and interesting. I'd trade a year of study nights for a night like that.

Ben could concentrate very deeply when studying, but he would always take time to chat if something was on my mind. Time wasn't important. If he could help someone, or create a new idea, this was well worth the hour lost in sleep.

For his honors thesis, Ben chose William Butler Yeats, which was perhaps the most enjoyable scholastic venture of his career. Insufficient time kept him from a final composition that met his own standards. In a call to his parents he said wearily, "Well, my thesis is in. But it won't get recognition. It isn't up to what I wanted to hand in."

Yet at Senior Chapel, Ben was announced as winning the Ralph

Waldo Rice Award. In the excitement he almost overlooked the one hundred dollar check included in the envelope with the citation.

This brief quotation from his thesis on Yeats provides a glimpse of the spirit of his maturing young mind.

> Yeats believed with Blake that all "imaginative art" was a "divine revelation." This clarifies the way in which Yeats meant to use the imagination to enter into the realm of the "eternal"— the world of "impossible purities" which Rossetti sought and tried to capture in the expression of a woman's face, where, as Yeats said, "the ecstasy of the lover and of the saint are alike, and desire becomes wisdom without ceasing to be desire."

At graduation time Ben was elected to Phi Beta Kappa and received his degree *magna cum laude*. His thesis received further citation from the English faculty as the finest paper submitted to the department for the year. But what pleased his parents most was the affection among students and faculty alike as they congratulated Ben on this achievement.

The Dean greeted the Symons warmly. "I know you are happy parents and you have cause to be. Your son did a wonderful job on the campus as in his studies. He has had a strong moral influence on his fellow students. I just wish we had a lot more like him."

Other members of the faculty expressed the same high praise in letters sent his parents a few months later after his tragic death.

Amherst, January 9, 1958

Dear Mr. and Mrs. Symon:

> It was a rare privilege to know Ben as a student and as a friend. He was completely dedicated to the search for truth in the fundamentals of life, and as a friend his complete honesty and unusual sensitivity enriched the lives of all who knew him.
>
> Sincerely,
> J. A. Martin, Jr.
> Department of Philosophy
> and Religion

Amherst, January 4, 1958

Dear Mr. and Mrs. Symon:

> I know that no matter how long my career may be, there will not be many students who will be able to come up to Ben. What

made him so outstanding was his mature seriousness of purpose, his conscientiousness and enthusiasm, his willingness to accept any amount of hard work and to face any challenge—and above all, a degree of intellectual honesty that I have rarely encountered. As his friend and as his teacher, I know what a remarkable, noble, genuine person Ben was, and how promising his future. . . .

Elmo Giodanetti
Department of Romance Languages

Amherst, December 23, 1957

Dear Mr. and Mrs. Symon:

Working with Ben on his thesis on Yeats last year was one of the pleasantest experiences I have had as a teacher. He was always genuinely concerned with the realities of the subject, never just trying to make a plausible argument. As the year went forward, his grasp of Yeats' meaning and his relation to the culture of his time became more and more profound, so that the essay he finally produced was among the best we have ever had. All the while Ben was so modest about what he was doing—so conscious of what he had not yet done, rather than what he had done.

He was always self-consistent, utterly honest, ready to change his mind and write off first thoughts in favor of more searching ones. His humor was part of his integrity and modesty; he was at once diffident and manly, a thoroughly lovable person.

Sincerely yours,
C. L. Barber
Department of English

The final days at Amherst were coming fast, but the close-knit friendships of mind and spirit and the memory of experiences shared would linger, as one of his classmates later expressed it:

The experiences we shared were all adventures—they meant a great deal because each of us had a sincere respect for the other man's strength. It was a continuity, a process of introspection, desire, and growth. In the traditional Senior Goat, a fraternity meeting in which the seniors all speak to the fraternity in parting, Ben said that to look on achievements as culminations would be to break the powers of life as a process of growth.

Ben's gifts were spent in giving. In that sense, each of us is a part of the others—and Ben Symon was, and is, a part of us all. So I hope you'll understand me when I say that Ben, for me and for the others, I'm sure, is not gone: he will live as long as we are alive, not only in our fondest memories, but as a part of the man in each and every one of us.

Ben was now planning on two years at Edinburgh instead of one. This meant four years of graduate study since two resident years were required at Yale Divinity School.

Anxious to share some of the expense, the summer of 1957 saw him working at a filling station on one of the busiest highways outside of New York City. The hours were long, the work monotonous. After the first days Ben was exhausted and said, "I marvel at how those fellows have been able to endure that job for years and still seem fairly content. If I don't make some sort of game out of it it'll get me."

He was concerned, as he came to see in his fellow workers the wide spread between opportunities and advantages. They all took their lunch as there was no place or time for a lunch hour. Ben, at times, left something special uneaten in his lunch box, and explained, "Mother, I feel embarrassed to eat before those fellows when there is such a difference. They remarked about my fried chicken and how their 'old lady' wouldn't cook like that for them. Their lunch is cold cuts—between white bread."

When Ben's job was ending he asked his mother to bake a cake for the men. He reported that evening, "The fellows sure liked that cake and were they *surprised!* They're real friends and I'm going to miss them. They taught me a lot." After Ben's death Mr. and Mrs. Symon visited the men at the station and were touched by the regard expressed for Ben. "Yes, we saw the terrible news in the paper. We've thought a lot about you folks."

From another, "We had a wonderful Christmas letter from Ben. Never knew a young fellow like him. Full of fun, but mighty serious too."

"He liked to talk to us and he sure said some fine things."

One of the men smiled as he said, "He told us all about him going to be a Priest—Preacher, you say. We called him 'Parson.' Ben liked that."

Yet another said, "You had a mighty good boy. Too bad there ain't more like him."

CHAPTER 6

Edinburgh

Ｄuring the summer of 1957, Ben corresponded with George Moses, his fraternity roommate who was going to Edinburgh with him. A letter of July 13th portrays his concerns:

Dear "Mo":

It occurs to me that during the past few weeks you may have thought *you* are holier than I. This unsavory idea may have been aroused by my seeming lack of response to your enlightening missile of June 24th last. But not a day has passed, "mon vieux" (this is French, which in your unenlightened state, you will undoubtedly not be able to comprehend) that I have not thought of thee. Unbelievably a free hour has now arrived, and the thought of you, George, yes, of you, was the first to leap in my mind. . . .

There isn't much variety to my job—pump gas, throw oil into the crankcase—all worthy tasks, contributing to the welfare of "mankind's noble estate!" Insignificant as it may seem, there is the sense of doing something that must be done. It is significant insofar as it is necessary. With the necessity goes responsibility which has to be fulfilled.

This is what makes work so important to the health of a community or personality. You can see it in the men around me. This is their job and they are doing it, not because it is world-shaking, but because of what the work means in terms of their responsibility to themselves and their families. It is their livelihood. To have a family and to sustain it with love and with the labor which is a part of that love—isn't this enough purpose for any man to have in life?

There is more, of course. The "higher" devotion to lofty ideals —abstractions like Truth with a capital "T." But what do these mean if they are not bred into the everyday demands which life sets before us? To recognize Truth in the abstract,—the glimmer of light on a dim, distant horizon is one thing. More important is to make our work a witness to what we believe.

One of the things that got me started on all of this was a movie I saw (be on the lookout for it) called "The Lost Continent." The idea is that the spiritual is not separate from the material. The Asians portrayed in it are so close to the facts of birth and death and the cycle which runs on a knife edge in between. Life for them is like an act of worship.

We are so used, in the west, to the tradition of the Holy Grail, the promised land beyond Jordan, apart from this life. We have progressed far in our knowledge of how to cope with the world and we have lost a sense of meaning in the miracle of life and death. Not that we should all decide to be peasants. It is only that progress seems to be both a blessing and a curse.

We strive with professional and technical skill to make birth and death and the days in between as easy as possible. The horror is that we may be making ourselves insensible to life itself.

I don't know what the fellows over at the station would think of all this. I do know, though that I am really taken with this notion of the separation between the spiritual and the material, between the religious and the secular, which seems somehow (and I think wrongly) to be a rule of our very existence. Why should it be so? There is a purity to this notion which seems to be at the heart of what makes a man a saint. What is compelling about Jesus is this mingling of the ideal with the practical situation, the immediate now. Everyone seems to agree that his gospel was not so much an ethic, as it was a life lived. I may be out to lunch, but it seems to me we are wrong in setting our spiritual life far away from what we do and think and say. If there is a Holy Grail, we ought to walk into the woods with Frost and find it, and make the connection between past and present.

Reading goes slowly, but I have managed to get through some interesting things—C. S. Lewis' *Surprised by Joy,* Levin's *Compulsion* (absorbing), *Anna Karenina,* and a little of Kierkegaard's *Fear and Trembling.*

Let me hear from you when you get a chance, which means, of course, immediately.

thy brother sy

P.S. How's the love life?

The destination of the following letter was a suburb of London, the home of relatives, where Ben and George planned to visit en route to Edinburgh:

Dear Cousin May,

We have been in the midst of moving for some time now, and
and we are just beginning to settle in our new surroundings—a
five-and-a-half room apartment about 2 miles from the house
which you visited. The job of squeezing the endless number of
things accumulated in a 13-room house over a 12-year period into
a small apartment is a challenging one. We stored a number of
things, but evidently not enough, for every room looks as if it
were a disorganized storeroom in a furniture store.

Thank you for your kind invitation to my friend, George Moses,
and myself. It is good of you to think of us. I only hope we will
not cause you too much inconvenience. Our plans are finally ar-
ranged, and include about a three-day stay in the London area.
We will dock in Southampton sometime on September 27th.

Mr. and Mrs. Symon had sold their home, planning to soon
move south. On the last day in the old home Ben said, "there's
been a lot of living here—I hate to leave this house where we've
all had so much happiness. This will always be home in my
memory, no matter where we live. I'm glad I have all the pictures
of the flowers."

A treasured bit of family humor surrounded Mrs. Symon's devotion to her garden. Ben delighted in teasing his mother, especially to guests: "We never know what to expect. Mother moves
shrubs like furniture. The entire garden can change in a day."

Finishing at the filling station, Ben made a hurried flight to
New Orleans to say goodbye to Bob and his family. On the last
evening before his departure he chatted with his mother: "It was
great to be with Bob and see how happy he is with Langston and
that adorable little Beth. But the time was too short." Then,
sadly, "I really don't know Bob, Mother—as brothers should. Do
you realize how little I have seen him in my lifetime?"

Mrs. Symon spoke cheerfully of future occasions when they
would all be together, and how the eight years difference in their
ages would disappear. Then she asked Ben to find a pleasing
Scottish name for the new home planned on the Gulf Coast. Ben's
mind seemed to be far away as he said, "I will think about it and
will so look forward to our being together. But two years is a long
time—and so much can happen."

Before he got into bed, Ben said, "I wish I had a small Bible
to carry. The pocket-sized books have given me many extra hours

of reading." Mrs. Symon gave him a small Testament in which she wrote "With love and prayers from mother as you begin your work for Christ in the land of your forebears. Faith, Hope and Love can conquer all things. September 20, 1957."

Then his mother kissed him. "I'll be kissing you goodnight every night. Love can leap the ocean in a split second, for God is its deliverer." Ben looked up. "Mother, there's so much I wanted to say to you and Dadden—but I can't find the words."

Early next morning, before leaving the apartment, Ben took a last look at the furniture he had helped arrange.

"Let me get a clear picture of everything. Then be sure to write me about any changes." Then, with a twinkle, "I know there will be a hundred moves before I see this apartment again. But don't you dare relocate that bookcase again," remembering the several times he had moved it in the past few days at his mother's direction.

At the boat Ben and George were thoughtful. Their mission ahead made light talk difficult. Pictures were taken. Conversation turned to Scotland and the plan to see the boys there in springtime when Mr. Symon was to make a business trip. They brightened at the thought of a leisurely vacation tour of Scotland and England with the Symons.

Mrs. Symon kissed George and said, "It means so much to us that you will be with Ben. Without you, I don't think I could let him go so far for such a long time." A plunge of the young man's Adam's apple told his feelings: "It means much to me to be with Ben, too."

As Mrs. Symon watched the ship fade into the mist she recalled all the near-tragedies in Ben's life and the times he made their hearts swell with pride and joy. She whispered her gratitude to God for all He had given their family through Ben.

There was a final ship-to-shore telephone call in the evening, the last time his parents heard Ben's voice: "Goodnight and lots of love to you both for now—and so-long."

An automobile, purchased before he left home as his graduation present, was waiting in London. Though Ben was feverish with Asian flu, he was able to manage English traffic customs and delivered himself and George at Stevenage. After three days of care, they were able to proceed to Edinburgh. But on the trip, George got the flu. It was a weary pair that reached the Scottish

boardinghouse which was to be their home during the ensuing
months.

The experiences of Ben during the weeks at Edinburgh are
best given in his own words. The following letters were written
to his family and intimate friends from shipboard and from his
new Scottish home.

> Aboard R.M.S. Nieuw Amsterdam
> Saturday, September 21, 1957

Dear S ——:

Just came out of church in the 1st Class theatre. A missionary
on his way back to Ceylon preached the sermon on what he
called "The true saving faith" of Shadrack, Mesack, and Abed-
nego. Aside from the fact that he addressed us all as "beloved"
(which being a matter of taste, I can overlook), I was not won by
his approach. What he was talking about—the difficulty of faith
and the all but impossible conditions of its demands—is certainly
a good subject—one which is explored thoroughly by Kierkegaard.
I did not care for his glib use of words like "true" and "saving," as
if their meaning was obvious and self-evident.

But it's one thing to be critical—to discriminate and accept as
well as reject—and another to be an intellectual snob. And after
all, how can I, any more than he, decide what is the whole story
and what is not? So if his approach is not acceptable to me, it is
to others; and since this is (like art) more a matter of taste than
of opinion (doctrine?) there is really no great issue. There are
many ways to climb the same mountain.

Interesting tidbit: Just found out that the German girl who sits
at our table is a baroness. Bones and I have decided that it is our
duty to show this girl a little more attention. After all, she is all
alone on the ship; and, since we are acquainted with her, we
would really be impolite if we didn't spend some time with her.
Besides, if we can get her address, we may be able to get her to
invite us to her house or castle, or whatever it is, in the Bavarian
Alps. I'm sure you understand our motives and heartily approve.

> Aboard R.M.S. Nieuw Amsterdam
> Thursday, September 26, 1957

Dear Mother and Dadden,

With all the leisure time on our hands, "Mo" and I have had
plenty of opportunity to take stock of what lies ahead of us. Conversation ranges from a discussion of the nature of faith to the
girl near to Mo's heart. For what it's worth, I feel now a "single-
ness of a purpose."

It is not a passive feeling of acceptance. It is much more of a calm determination to dive headlong into the stream of whatever lies ahead. I feel a sense of purpose—not that I don't have doubts. I feel convinced that faith is not something gained and maintained on an even level throughout our lives. What we believe in comes in instants, not once, but many times, and in different ways, and under many different circumstances. These come and go, with a burst of emotion and an urgency about them. Faith is not something learned nor given by one's upbringing or environment. Rather is it given, if it is given at all, by something completely beyond our power to understand or control. It is something completely personal, and it becomes quite simply and without question the power and passion of our lives.

*I am not talking about the dramatic certainly of a flash of lightning from the sky—the kind of thing described in the changing of Saul to Paul on the road to Damascus. (There are few so blessed.) What I am talking about are those rare, momentary glimpses of the road which we must take and of the things which we must do—such moments when our souls are so moved with conviction that there is no room in our minds for any rational judgment, room for no other sensation than that of complete and utter self-surrender. These are moments which break upon us unexpectedly, and which leave us as suddenly as they come, and afterwards we are always in search of them. What we have thus seen is no longer a part of the present, but is a part of our memoried selves, and we are forever trying to recapture what we have known. How do we try? Simply by living: By setting our minds and hands to this and that task with this and that rational conviction about what we are doing: by living our lives within some sort of pattern: by living FOR something—for "love," for "faith" —whatever words we want to use to name it. But there is always the "for," always the purpose and the line of search—not that we ever put these things into words as I am trying to do now. But we do care "for" something. When you get right down to it, our very lives themselves are testimony to those things which we do care for.

It is not an easy thing to grasp hold of. It is always elusive, always on the wing, never a "sure thing." It is not a matter of telling yourself that you believe thus and so; for if you look deeply enough within yourself, you know that what you say you believe is hardly acceptable, hardly possible. Faith—"the essence of things hoped for, the evidence of things not seen," says Hebrews 11:1. This is it—daring to believe the impossible. The vision (or

---

* Italics by L.R.D.

whatever) leads us after it, more compelled than motivated. The agony of this belief and doubt is never far from the convictions of faith. At any rate, this is my situation now.

My unsettled state must seem a little vague and uncalled for. I know you are right and that I shouldn't bother myself so much. (I am a born worrier, and I think I always will be.) *The trouble is I don't want to slide into the ministry. I want to do it with a sense of undivided and certain commitment. Doubt may be an enemy, but it cannot be put aside. It is just as real as faith. And so here I stand; I will simply have to dive in and see where I come out.*

Up early tomorrow to check out. Goodbye Nieuw Amsterdam, hello plaid land.

Love,
Goody

P.S. If you are thinking that George would be a big help to me in my rather confused state, think again. He is more confused than I am! We are truly "the blind leading the blind." At least it's exciting.

Wednesday, October 2, 1957

Dear Cousin May,

I hope by now you are well on the way to recovery from the sudden bad turn you took last Sunday. I'm afraid you took quite a beating from our visit, and I am sorry we couldn't commend you properly, before we left, for your magnificent courage. You all deserve a gold star for looking after such a wayward twosome as George and myself. And I cannot tell you how sorry I am for the inconvenience (and ultimate misery) caused you by my being sick. Illness is certainly as unpleasant for those around the patient as for the patient himself, especially in this case, where plans were disrupted and we could not chat and become better acquainted. I want you to know, though, that I am especially grateful for your wonderful care. I don't know what I would have done without the comfort and warmth of what I already feel is my home away from home in the British Isles.

George and I are now more or less settled in and find ourselves snugly fitted into a room that is not nearly so large as we imagined in our mind's eye. Our biggest difficulty is study space. We have no desks and no likely prospect of finding any. Besides, even if we did have them, there is really nowhere to put them. Mrs. Whitelaw's only other boarder is a bacteriologist working on his Ph.D. He has his books and equipment at the laboratory where he is doing his research. He leaves all his things there and does not try to do any studying at his digs. This, I suppose, Mrs. Whitelaw assumed we would do. However, the only study facilities we will have access to will be those in the library at the college, which closes at 5 p.m. We can go along to the public library till 9; but this is really no great help, for in any case we are left with no study nook to call our own.

We only had a single bed between us in Newcastle on Monday night. You can well imagine the tussle between us over the blankets. I think George came out the next morning a little the worse for wear, for he had taken a chill during the night and became progressively worse as the day went on. As soon as he hopped into the double bed at Mrs. Whitelaw's, however, he seemed to feel an immediate improvement, and by morning he was up and ready to go into town. And to top it all off, I felt so sorry for him when we arrived (he said he could hardly stand) that I carried his big suitcase (ask Moyra how heavy it is) all sixty-four stone steps to our flat on the top floor. There has to be poetic justice, and for George it must be waiting just around the corner.

Edinburgh
October 3, 1957

Rolling toward Newcastle on Monday evening, we were on a height overlooking a shallow valley showing the outskirts of the city. It was raining, but the sun was just setting. All the houses in the valley, the hills, and even the horizon itself—were shrouded in a sea of mist which made sky and earth seem one. Sounds fray —and it would have been, except for the setting sun. Shining through the mist and dust, it highlighted surfaces in the valley making them glow with reddish light; and the air was turned into a brilliant kind of haze.

The English countryside is as green as anything I've ever seen before and it gives you the comfortable feeling of things stable and familiar and made to show their best. Not that it's "familiar" to me. Though the hedgerows, clipped and bushy, run for miles in place of fences, you rarely feel the sense of space as you do in the States.

But now we are in Edinburgh—gray, with soot-blackened walls and smoke-filled streets, and high old buildings casting long blue shadows across splotches of watery sunlight. This is the look of the old part of the city where we are. Plenty of cobbled streets and horse-drawn milk carts. This morning I saw my first kilt-clad gentleman, striding across the "meadows"—the all-purpose patch of green near where we are—complete with bushy mustache, walking-stick, and tam. Seeing him march by gave me a start, and I braced up my shoulders and became excitingly aware that I was in Scotland.

Our room is done in kind of light tan or dun color, with long green curtains flanking two rather large and drafty windows on one side wall. Another wall has a fireplace and mantel in the middle of it, on the hearth of which we have our handy-dandy electric "radiator" (heater, that is) which communicates the warmth of its personality to us for the nominal fee of one shilling (14¢) every five-and-one-half hours. Already it is cold, and in the mornings when I step out of bed, I think my little toe is going to break off. For the last two days, before our trunks came, I have been walking around with no overcoat, and with pajamas on under a pair of summer slacks. I'm afraid by the time winter comes, I will be putting on clothes to go to bed, rather than taking them off.

We go up today to hear the opening lecture (to all students) at New College. On my first visit the caretaker sent me off toward a huge door across the inner court, and said that if I went in I should find the librarian. As I crossed the court, cordovans sounding loudly on the cobbled pavement, three stories of bleak-looking classroom windows loomed all around me, and I was aware of the watchful eye of John Knox, looking down upon me from his pedestal to the left. I reached the door—heavy wood paneling studded with great iron bolts—and pulled it open. It was dim and musty—not a sound. I felt like I was in an abandoned inner keep of some old castle. A stone staircase spiraled up to my right, and there was a sign saying "Library." I went up slowly and with an odd feeling in the pit of my stomach. What could I possibly have to do with a place like that? I thought to myself, here are recorded ages of thought. It is the seat of a tradition, but where is the life? How will I be able to come into touch with it?

The door at the top of the stairs was locked. As no one answered my knock, I wandered back down to a landing and along a little narrow corridor to a door marked "Sanctuary." I stepped inside and found myself in a narrow little sliver of a room, filled with rows of chairs and punctuated by a stained glass window and altar looking down from the other end. Crowded against the wall was a little hand organ. The room seemed so empty—so hidden and out-of-the-way that I felt as if I had stumbled upon something long forgotten. I felt like an intruder, a stranger, who had yet a great deal to learn about the worship of God. New College is going to pick me up and show me so much that I need to know. I can't wait to see the place come alive and hear the men speak.

Hot lunch coming up, and if there's anything hot to be had, you've got to hurry because it doesn't stay that way very long.

The life in Edinburgh was described with charm and humor to family and friends in the midst of a heavy schedule of study and activity.

> 12 Leven Terrace
> Edinburgh, Scotland
> October 5, 1957

Dear F——:

The men at New College seem bound together by the strength of a tradition much older than themselves. (They all wear robes to class, for one thing.) They have at once the assurance and humility of men who have seen the truth and they are excited. They want to tell you all about it. I think the time spent here is going to see more of a significant change in "yours truly" than I can even now imagine. This place will either claim me or beat me into the ground. I have many doubts about all that lies ahead. I suppose though I always will; and, having reconciled myself to this, I want to go ahead as quickly as I can and see how it all turns out. It should make a good story.

Last night I slipped and told Mrs. Whitelaw I thought Mo and I would "hit the sack early." You should have seen the expression on her face! She didn't know what I was talking about. Today at lunch we had a delicious apple dish for dessert. We were all commenting on how good it was, and then I started it off by asking her what she called it. "Why that's apple crundy," she answered. "It's just the same as our deep dish apple pie," I replied, and thought the matter was closed. "No, that's apple betty," pipes up Mo. "Apple what?" asks Mrs. Whitelaw. "We call it apple charlotte in New Zealand," says our other friend. "Now, wait a minute," says George, paying no attention to Mrs. Whitelaw, "This is pretty sweet, so it's probably Apple-pan-doughty." Along the way we touched on apple cobbler, apple tart, and apple crunchy. Mrs. Whitelaw is a trusting soul, but she just couldn't keep a straight face throughout all this. We all broke up and agreed in the end that it had been a "ripping" meal. Well, we're learning; and maybe by the time we come back we will have mastered the Highland fling and the Scottish brogue.

The most wonderful thing I know is touching another person; and I am coming to think more and more that whatever we may know of "ultimates" is to be found in the miracle of such wonders as friendship and love. Thank God for the trust that makes two people talk and understand each other as we have. I will always be grateful to you for the many things said and done in that most understanding way of yours.

Ben

The more serious side is dealt with, too.

October 8, 1957

Dear S——:

I must describe for you the closed communion service held for the ninety-some-odd students of New College in the spacious quietness of St. Giles Cathedral. I wish you could have felt, as did I, the meaningfulness of this experience. Picture us, first of all, entering singly and in pairs into the dimly lit nave of the great church, whose origin is forgotten in some prehistoric time. The organist plays, but it only emphasizes the quiet, which seems to hang suspended between each footfall that is made. Above our heads, in the slim vault of the nave, hang the tattered remnants of ancient Scottish battle flags, ghostly reminders of the ideals which have fired the breasts of other men in other times. You feel as if you are walking on holy ground, among spirits who have lived the passionate reality of suffering and self-sacrifice.

As you gather with the other students in the stolid-looking choir stalls in the chancel, you become increasingly aware of those who stand in this present moment with you. For you are part of a community brought together in a common spirit of dedication and devotion to something that lies at the heart of being itself. You know you are all facing the moment of sacrifice, the challenge inherent in the demand of life itself. The dying in order to live, which you feel welling up out of all the tradition of this church suddenly is a present reality.

As the Dean of New College, Professor Burleigh, begins quietly to speak of the love of God and the nearness of Christ in this symbolic recognition of his sacrifice, you feel very humble, and you want to pray and re-dedicate yourself in the spirit of His supreme act of self-sacrifice. You feel weak and you pray for strength; you feel joyful and within your heart you cry out your thanks. And in the back of your mind, you feel doubtful, uncertain of your faith and your steadfastness. Yes, they are all there—

all the conflicting elements of your soul—all laid bare in this humble giving of yourself. And finally as you take the bread and the wine, symbols of the sacrifice, you feel the meaning of God's Grace, the strength which stands in the place of your weakness. You walk away waiting and hoping and yes, believing, but above all, determined to try and try again.

Edinburgh
October 9, 1957

Dear S——:

Just returned from my weekly French class at the French institute here in the city. An hour a week of conversation to keep me in practice, and I'm in sad need of it. What's it like? Well, we all sit around in a tight little circle (about fifteen strong) and listen to our leader ask us questions about the sights of the city. Since I know little about this place as yet, I was able to get by tonight with an occasional "Je ne sais pas." I am amazed at how much I have lost. It is hearing the language that counts, and I have simply lost touch with the sound and the syntax. (On this score, I am very continental "savoir faire.")

The classroom atmosphere over here is different from any I have known previously. Every lecture is preceded and ended with a prayer and benediction. Every word and thought with which we have to do seems steeped in common assumptions. . . . I am afraid I am not yet thoroughly enough "indoctrinated" with these assumptions to feel at ease in the atmosphere. Not that I do not feel inspired by the prayers themselves, for they are usually expressions of humility in the common search for truth. But I feel hemmed in by the word "God" as if all that takes place between Prayer and Benediction is somehow parenthetical; and as if I have been chosen before I have myself made a choice. I feel now as if my understanding will always be incomplete until I have "decided" and placed myself within the inner circle of knowledge conferred by faith. (This way of sizing things up I borrow from today's lecture on the words of St. Anselm: "I believe in order to understand"—or more authentically in the Latin, "Credo ut intelligam.")

Time was taken in innumerable relationships to express personal affection, concern or helpfulness. Characteristic is the following note of sympathy sent to the mother of a friend whose husband had died.

12 Leven Terrace
Edinburgh, Scotland
October 12, 1957

Dear Mrs. N_____:

I have just learned of the great loss that is yours; and though words can say very little, I want you to know that my deepest sympathies are with you and all your family.

It is hard for me to express my feelings. I cannot say that I share *your* sorrow, for no one outside yourselves can taste the full measure of that. But I do want to pay my respects to a man for whom I felt a great deal of admiration.

I felt the strength of his character and what I can only call the high discipline of his spirit.

My thoughts and sympathies are with you all.

Most sincerely,
Ben Symon

Mrs. Whitelaw proved to be a wonderful friend, as well as landlady, in providing a warm "second home" for the young man from America. Ben's tender concern for other people is reflected in his description of her:

Edinburgh
October 13, 1957

Dear Mother and Dadden,

I have still an awful lot to get used to. Like "tea" for instance. I have never drunk so much of the stuff in my life. I used to associate it with an upset stomach, and at first I felt as if I ought to be sick to merit all this attention. We have tea for breakfast, at mid-morning break at school, for lunch, for supper and at bedtime. Last Sunday I had nine cups with an extra two cups at a church youth meeting. I suppose when it gets a little colder I'll appreciate it more.

Our situation with Mrs. Whitelaw is working out well. You remember the two categories of landlady types—the motherly type and the all-business type? Mrs. Whitelaw comes under category number one. She's a good cook (we have not had the same dessert twice since we've been here, and they've all been good) and if she wants to be "motherly" in this respect, who are we to complain? She is a very lonely person. She lost her husband just a year ago after nursing him for seven years. He was struck suddenly with some type of paralysis and, after attacks over a period of a few years, lapsed into a complete helplessness. During the last three years he was unable to speak. It was all a pretty terrible experience for her, especially as they had no children and no one to help them with the financial burden. All of his savings were used up and she now has to depend entirely on boarders to support herself. She is trying to adjust to the entirely new situation in which she finds herself. Needless to say, we are part of this new situation.

Douglas Dye (whom I think I told you about) is the only other boarder here and is a prince of a fellow, about 30, with a wife and two children back in New Zealand. He came here just after Mr. Whitelaw passed away and has been a godsend for Mrs. Whitelaw. Now that we are here, she has more to keep her busy and is glad for our company as well as the added income.

The capacity to "enfold" any experience with full-orbed attention and delight is revealed in the following letters to a close friend:

Edinburgh
October 13, 1957

I am now bursting with the news of something wonderful. George and I have just come from church where we heard one of the most thrilling affirmations I have ever heard. A Gaelic-Scotch minister by the name of MacDonald made us feel, as I have rarely felt before, the reality of the religious situation in the whole span of human existence. I cannot hope to convey any of the impact of his message in a letter, but I would like to try.

His text was taken from II Kings 6:8-17. In this passage is related the story of Elisha and a young man, his servant, who are "encompassed about" by a great band of Syrians. The young man is afraid. "What shall we do?" he cries to Elisha, who replies calmly, "Fear not, for those who be with us are more than those who be with them." Then, with a dramatic gesture—"Open your eyes that you may see"—he reveals to the young man a vision of the Host of Heaven—horses and chariots of fire felling the mountain. This was the beginning and I wondered where in the world he was going. Here was one of those "flick of the wrist" Biblical miracles that made you feel uncomfortable. But he jumped from here right into the heart of our modern situation. "Can't we say," he said in effect, "that the situation of Elisha is similar to that of the Christian Church today? Christianity on the defensive? Are we not now, perhaps more than ever before 'encompassed about' by an 'intellectual assurance that Christianity is a part of a mythical conception of experience that is now completely outdated, and by a world that is fast losing its aura of mystery?' Look at your churches. Most people really don't care what goes on inside them.

Where is religion today? It is fighting a losing battle, and it might just as well throw in the sponge."

I was excited, because the man was speaking to us (he never used a note) about things which we all knew to be the truth. He then went on to affirm that religion, or the religious sensibility, lies at the very heart of the human situation, and that the vision of Elisha revealed to the young man in doubt the "allies of the soul"—the inner sensibilities that are part of every man in doubt in every age. He went on to enumerate them as (1) the sense of moral guilt, which, he said, has been the main theme of every major literary work that has ever been written—from *Oedipus Rex* to T. S. Eliot's *Cocktail Party;* (2) the awareness of truth (in whatever context, be it science or theology) and man's ultimate recognition of it; (3) the challenge and comfort of the truth as it is revealed to us; (4) man's hunger for the divine, his reaching out for that which he knows lies beyond his power to understand or control, but which he needs to make his life complete.

As he spelled these things out, he made them jump from the narrow context of our words about God and Christ in the theological sense—and made them relevant.

What MacDonald had to say fell into line with a sentence of Jacques Maritain I ran across the other day, to wit: "under many names, names which are not that of God, in ways known only to God, the interior act of a soul's thought can be directed towards a reality which in fact truly may be God"—which says that even a so-called "atheist" may know God and believe in God, even though he may himself emphatically deny that this is the case.

MacDonald ended up with the story of a hard-bitten, swaggering hero type he had known in a prisoner of war camp. He was contemptuous of religion until he got hold of Lloyd Douglas' *The Robe,* and read it through one night. "If what *The Robe* says is true," this man said to MacDonald, "then my whole life has been a ghastly mockery." Said MacDonald, "I am well aware that there are many valid criticisms of a book like *The Robe.* I am sure that I could write a devastating critical review of it and that I would be right in doing so. The fact remains, however, that this book touched the heart and soul of one man, and as it did so what was not the Word of God *became* the Word of God."

George and I both felt as if a tremendous affirmation has been made. It is nothing new of course, but is something which ought to be kept clearly before us, and especially before the Church which is the rightful guardian and interpreter of Theology. Theology is all-important to the Church, whose function it is to witness to the Truth—to preach the Gospel—but it is never itself the

Gospel, never itself, the word; for the Word of God comes to men not as men will have it come, but whenever and however it will, and as Maritain says, "under many names." If Jesus really is Christ, then He has confronted men in every age, no matter what the words of explanation or description. I firmly believe (as Yeats puts it) that "We know much we do not know." God is a reality in our lives whether we know it or not. Jesus Christ, though we meet Him historically in a certain time and in a certain place, is not confined in His action upon our lives to any time or to any place.

Edinburgh
October 20, 1957

Arising at an early hour and enjoying a hearty breakfast, we greeted the dawn of a bright Saturday morning and hopped into our green bugmobile and scooted with three friends to the ferry and across the Firth to the coast road heading along the jut of land known as "fife."

I clambered out along some rocks to get a picture by the hamlet of St. Monance, and as I stood mid-way between headstones of a tiny graveyard and sea, I had a curious sense of Time-suspended. Everything seemed to stop, even my thoughts insofar as I was aware of them, and the whole moment seemed one—sea and sky, church and rocks, the sound of the sea and the silence of my heart. But it was all just for a moment, and all without these words; and then I raised my camera and took my picture. But now as always, these things take on a greater significance in the mind's eye, and I see the scene as something other than it was on the surface—a kind of revelation? A nice theological question: the nature of revelation. Can you have revelation with a capital "R" in a sunset as well as in Jesus Christ? This is one of those "ultimate" unanswerable questions we've been dealing with these days. It's odd how almost everything I do ends up by being considered in the light of this kind of question. . . . A day like yesterday comes so rarely over here, that when it does come it suffuses your heart with joy and thanksgiving that makes you realize how lucky you are to have the enjoyment of such things as sunshine and countryside trees.

We finally arrived at St. Andrews, city of twelve thousand, father of the sporting game of golf, and quadrangled shelter of many thousands of students since the founding of its university in 1413. It's a quiet town, with little green walks and parks tucked away behind buildings dating back as far as the 16th century. At one end of the town there are the remains of a medieval

cathedral which fell into ruin after the Reformation, when the
worthy church fathers no longer felt the need of such extravagant
display of their religious fervor. Places like this always give me a
little shiver. You always feel the impact of the passage of time. At
your feet is grass growing, and towering over you are the walls
crumbling.

Nowadays when a few of the boys over at the University get
a buzz on, they come over to the cathedral at night and dare each
other to climb the twin towers which are still standing at the
chancel end, and one of them actually did it. Over to one side
stands another smaller tower—all that is left of a small 11th century chapel. Duncan suggested we walk up to the top, and so we
paid a few pence and started up a dim, narrow staircase, spiraling
steeply up the dark well of this tower. At one point we had to
duck a huge supporting beam which is said to have come from the
wreck of one of the Spanish Armada ships. Above we heard the
voices of those descending. It would be a tight squeeze—hardly
any room to pass. Around the corner of this steep spiral, almost
directly over my head peeps the pert little face of Cindy Pratt
with Gerry coming along close behind. "Cindy," I say. "Hi," she
says, with no change of expression, simply answering her name;
and then, "Ben!" You could have knocked us both over with a
feather. What a place to meet! Squeezed together in the staircase
of an 11th century church tower! After the initital surprise had
had time to register, we began to talk and then to laugh, for our
situation really was ridiculous. So we squeezed by and let them
go, and then met them later for about an hour during tea time.

To another friend of long years' standing, Ben wrote, revealing
one of his finest graces—that of balance. He could engage in such
serious speculation and introspection that one might wonder if
the scales were a bit out of balance. But then would flow from his
nature a wonderful realism and down-to-earth practicality.

> 12 Levin Terrace
> Edinburgh, Scotland
> October 24, 1957

Dear C_____:

We are about 15 minutes' walk from New College and very
conveniently located for things like opera (saw *La Traviata* and
La Bohême last week—*Bohême* was great!), ballet (the Royal
Ballet this week-end), and movies—and oh yes, a walk in the park,
which is right outside our building.

The window cleaner came today, but he might just as well have stayed away because he can't do anything about the air, which is filled with the smoke of countless chimneys belching forth all over the city. The haze is never absent even on the brightest days, and it settles into all the alleyways, and lingers at every street corner.

I have walked into New College, and I have met a challenge, the like of which I have never met before. There is that part of us which is always fighting against what is demanded of us. The question is, how strongly do we feel the demand, and in what way? "Where shall we go that we may bow down and worship Him?" I think, too, that I'm too full of myself these days. I must begin to look out a little more. I'm going to a mission project in the slum area every week. It's going to do me a lot of good.

In letters from Ben during the Edinburgh experience, he reported that some of his questions were finding an answer in his study of the historical Jesus. Kierkegaard's idea of "becoming" a Christian, rather than "being" a Christian once and for all, had been a significant concept to Ben for several years.

> Edinburgh
> October 28, 1957

There is a discipline here different and more challenging than what I knew at Amherst. There is freedom—no quizzes or specified assignments to make you feel the pressure of something outside yourself. I read more or less when I want and as fast as I want, with plenty of time to take excursions into related topics of interest which are not specifically assigned. . . .

My malady is in my own inability to associate myself with beliefs which are taken for granted, or ones that are made to appear no longer open for discussion. It seems to me that the questions raised by the Christian challenge are always open for discussion, and that they can never be truly decided (even by the Holy Spirit working in us) unless they are kept open.

Belief is not a static thing. It has to do with modes of thought and action which are at the very heart of our "being in the world." I cannot accept the idea of something decided once and for all (and this is where I cannot see eye to eye with Billy Graham's presentation of the Gospel). . . .

A lot of my wonderings are beginning to be answered by a renewed acquaintance with the historical Jesus; and although it may sound as if I am reacting unfavorably to all the "newness," just exactly the opposite is true. There is no place I would rather be right now than here in Edinburgh. These questions have got to be answered, and I can think of no better place to do it.

I will be thinking of you in the preparation for Advent. This will be the first time I will have missed a Christmas Pageant in many a year. If luck holds, though, I should be in Scandinavia for the holidays. It will not be any substitute for home, but I am looking forward to it.

With all best regards,
Ben Symon

Ben admits that some of his letters are more of a monologue than a conversation, and yet in his candid, probing expression, one feels that he is coming ever closer to the alpha and omega of his quest.

Edinburgh
October 30, 1957

Here's a quick run-down on the day's activities. Awake at 7:15 with a mumble to George to shut off the alarm. He does. A gray and chilly dawn. Pop a shilling in the slot, on with the heater, a dash for the john, where three of us usually converge at once. In to breakfast and the comment of the day—"Ah, 'tis a gai (pronounced as in 'guy') dricht day." By 8:45 we're studying in our room, where we stay until about 9:30, then a couple of classes (maybe three) interspersed with "prayers" at 11:00 A.M.; and finally lunch in a little puddle of light.

Home again for supper where we banter our way through an excellent meal. This very pleasant ritual is always brought to a close by George "scraping out" the dessert bowl (which means he takes up his spoon to claw out every last crumb that is left). The rest of the evening is usually spent in studying, at least until 9:30 or so, when we are apt to dash around the corner to the nearest pub where we stay until closing time at 10:00. Then home for a "cup of tea" and an early sack around 11:30. It's a pleasant life allowing for all kinds of variation. Today, for instance, we didn't come right home at all, but went instead to the Royal Scottish Academy where we took in a really fine exhibition of paintings by Jack Yeats (brother of W.B.). Their fascination (and this is the only word for it) derives in part from their sensitive treatment of the commonplace. His style is impressionistic, a pilgrimage into the visionary world of the artist, who, like his brother, saw all things as somehow "other than they are." His subjects are mostly scenes from his Irish country life, but they are transformed by his original use of color—mingling the fire of passion and exhilaration with the softer hues of simple delights: two boys tumbling on a beach, light and shade, sea and sky and coast, all are mingled in a spontaneous impression—a visionary moment.

Edinburgh
November 5, 1957

I am still caught up in the after-glow of a thrilling experience, and I simply have to talk about it. Today at noon I attended the third in a series of lectures entitled "The Poets' Vision." The lectures are given in the assembly hall of a local church just over the hill from New College by W. B. J. Martin, minister of said church. The idea is to show, first of all, that religion, in the words of Paul Tillich, "is not a special function of man's spiritual life, but is the dimension of depth in all of its functions," and to show also how much of modern poetry is a religious commentary on the human situation which it portrays. This by way of introduction is dry, I know, but please bear with me.

Remember the subways?—the awful, self-conscious sense of being alone with nothing particular to think about, staring across the gulf between you and those along the other side of the car, one among many who gaze blankly out for fear of looking in, nameless, faceless, hopeless. . . .

"Or, as, when an underground train in the tube, stops too long
        between stations
And the conversation rises and slowly fades into silence
And you see behind every face the mental emptiness deepen
Leaving only the growing terror of nothing to think about. . . ."

So T. S. Eliot. The loss of personality, both conscious and unconscious. We play a part before the world, hoping to make the team, to be accepted and to count for something. This is our search, and it is a frantic one—a search for identity, for something with which we can identify ourselves—our words our thoughts our deeds. The man who sits behind a desk is lost when you take away the desk, for he is left without the necessary prop to successfully play his part. And here we have it—in this very sentence —"The man who sits behind the desk." Who is he? we ask. Why, he's a business man. But that is no answer. We have asked for a *name* and we received a *label*. The "who" has been swallowed up by the "it. . . ."

Then the time is lost. And for what? Do we know? Can we say? Remember how we used to laugh over what we had forgotten the week before? After an all but vain attempt to recall the course of events over the past weeks, we could invariably shelve the whole issue with something along the line of "Oh, the same routine," or "nothing in particular." If there is any meaning here, it is an ominous tragic one. For we simply cannot allow the particular to dissolve into "nothing in particular." It is the particular to which we must give ourselves, for it is only here that we can ever hope to find ourselves. But now I'm getting bogged down again by abstractions. Where is the life that we have lived and now lost in the past? And what is the present, what we do and think now in these moments, if the past is lost in Sheol, the "land of forgetfulness?" When the Psalmist cries out in despair to the Lord, he is calling for the self that is lost in darkness, in forgetfulness.

> "I am shut in so that I cannot escape:
>   my eye grows dim through sorrow. . . .
> Are thy wonders known in the darkness,
>   or thy saving help in the land of forgetfulness?"

Recovery of the self—the innocence and the delight of childhood, or of the passion for life which makes the soul surge in a moment of gladness. Easy enough to say, but we cannot find recovery in words. Where is the center of our being—that part that is lost in the "deep-buried, memoried self" of all the ages? Where can we discover life that does not turn to dust? . . . The lover sings to his love, "Love has no ending. . . ."

> "I'll love you dear, I'll love you
>   Till China and Africa meet
> And the river jumps over the mountain
>   and the salmon sings in the street. . . .
>
> But all the clocks in the city
>   begin to whir and chime:
> 'O let not time deceive you,
>   You cannot conquer Time.'
>
> In the burrows of the Nightmare
>   Where justice naked is,
> Time watches from the shadow
>   And coughs when you would kiss.
>
> In headaches and in worry
>   Vaguely life leaks away,
> And Time will have his fancy
>   Tomorrow or today. . . .
>
> O plunge your hands in water,
>   plunge them up to the wrist:
> Stare, stare in the basin
>   And wonder what you've missed. . . ."

(Snatches from Auden's song, "As I Walked Out One Evening.")

But now what is the point of all this? Here is poetry focusing on our common dilemma. If this is a religious statement, it is certainly a negative one. Where is there any room in this maze of all our days for any kind of positive affirmation? It is certainly not to be found in any kind of proposition about life in general, or even about life "in particular." The answer, when we find it (or it finds us) is to be found in life itself. We must go on living and we must go on meeting situations and people in situations as they arise.

The lecture today was pertinent to this point. It was on a poet by the name of Edwin Muir. He is a Scotsman who began to write poetry when he was thirty-five. It was for him the answer to what he called the need in every man to live his life "twice over," to rediscover the self as a person in relation to the other persons. During the course of his life he underwent psychoanalytic treatment, but broke it off on the advice of his analyst when it was discovered that his dreams and phantasies were so pregnant with half-seen implications that it was impossible to deal with them adequately. The experience was prolonged enough, however, to give Muir a profound sense of shame and self-disgust. "For I realized," he says in his autobiography, "that I was one with all of human-kind—that I shared with all men the same hopes and fears, the same secret lusts and twisted desires." The upshot of this was his poetry, which is his effort to throw light on the limbo of his inner self—not in a self-indulgent, plaintive tone—but in the spirit of a courageous effort to come to terms with his own personality, and with the "personality" of every man in every age in what Jung calls the "collective unconscious," a kind of repository of psychic patterns which recur in men down through the ages.

What thrilled me about this lecture was the resemblance between Muir's conception of himself as a poet and that of Yeats. The notion of "recovery of self" is common in both. And if Jung talks about the "collective unconscious," Yeats had his *"spiritus mundi"* and his "Great Memory of Nature." This was not the climax though. What really swept me off my feet (from which precarious position I commenced to write this brief note) was the way in which I re-discovered sensibility—the dramatic relation between self and self—is absolutely essential to the minister for his message. Sermons within a closed system of theological propositions about life or about God are no longer possible. We must "recover" the Biblical sense of a "way of life." We must speak, not about Christ, but from the standpoint of those in dynamic relation to Christ. Theological discussion is part of the necessary effort of faith to understand itself. It is not, however, the word of God; nor can it be proclaimed as such.

This has not been a very enjoyable letter to read, I know. Try to understand that I was excited and had to talk to someone on paper. I know it has been more of a monologue than a conversation, but I am sending it along for whatever it is worth. There is something unfinished about all this, something not quite grasped, not quite understood. I know, though, that poetry is an attempt to make some kind of order out of chaos of the mind and heart. We must learn to look into the heart of darkness that is our inner self, for it is only here that we can see the point of light that is buried deep within us. We must explore our memory, the past that shelves off into the inner deep of the subconscious; and, in whatever ways we can, draw out the moments of truth that are concealed. Read over I Cor. 13:8-13—those familiar words about the nature and preeminence of Love, and about the child becoming a man. . . .

"For now (as adults) we see in a mirror dimly, but then (as children) face to face." . . . *The re-discovery of the self . . . being 'born again' . . . the uncovering of that which we have known and still know, but have forgotten . . . And what is this mystical something? I don't know, but I am convinced it has something to do with our relation to something which is at once part of us and separate from us. The very fact of the age-long human search for self-fulfillment is enough to indicate this. We long for that which we have lost, and our very lives are urgent callings for rediscovery.*

And if we seek, then we shall find . . . in the quiet time . . . The time when time itself is still . . . the incredulous moment, when two become one . . . the seeker and the sought . . . the crisis of submission . . . life come to an end, and born again.

I know this is a puzzle. I read it over myself, and I hardly know what to make of it. It is probably more than a little incoherent—the rough data of a mood, rather than a coherent train of thought. If it shows anything, it is the crying need for a bit of self-discipline in my thought. So I do not blame you if you can't even finish reading it all. I am stammering, and I know it, but I know somehow that I am on the right track. . . . *There's so much, so terribly much, for us to learn about ourselves and about the whys and wherefores of what we do. It seems an endless task and so it is, but it is exciting and rewarding so long as we do not lose sight of the life that is ours to live.* . . .

---

* Italics by L.R.D.

From the deep probing for what we have lost and the "crisis of submission," there are earthy observations:

Edinburgh
November 8, 1957

By all ordinary standards I ought to be miserable—stuck in this dismal place, inhabited by sober red-faced folk (and the women *all* seem to have thick ankles—there's hardly a well-turned one among the lot) going efficiently about their business. But I find this place absolutely fascinating. In the first place, there is a lot to do—opera, ballet, concerts, lectures, etc.—and all at a very *cheap* price. So far I have seen two operas and a ballet and we will go Wednesday to see Laurence Olivier in *The Entertainer,* which is the latest from John ("The Angry Men") Osborne.

Then, the city, while outwardly cheerless and dismal, has charm —misty, chimney-potted, steeple-spired silhouettes, stretching away against the reddish haze of an evening sun that never quite shows itself. But most important is the university life. . . .

I am convinced the truest words I've run across are contained in the confession of one who says that Philosophy, while valuable and indeed necessary, is really no more than a process through which we persuade ourselves of that which we already believe before we start. A man's philosophy should be a kind of "autobiography."

There are so many thoughts and fleeting impressions running through my mind, that I hardly have time to catch them all, much less retain and write them down. I know we change from day to day, and we continually renew our lives with new thoughts, new decisions. . . .

I tell myself every day—"Listen to every voice that is within you; and do not take any leap until (or unless) all are tuned to the impulse that you feel." We must present ourselves in all that we do.

All the best,
Ben

Edinburgh
November 11, 1957

. . . There are more book stores in the city than I have seen anywhere else. Books are cheap and easy to come by—a gold mine for anyone interested in building up his own library. Then there are the coffee houses tucked away in little corners all about the city, where students habitually gather and huddle over their cups of tea—they are all rather intense, about what I don't know. You see lots of pipes, puffing furiously, and a lot of beards and mustaches; but when you speak to them, you find more often than not that you are tuning in on a familiar drawl or twang and are talking to someone who shouldn't misuse, as he is, the freedom he has.

As the days moved into December, Ben and his friend, George Moses, made plans for a holiday trip to Scandinavia, about which Mr. and Mrs. Symon raised serious questions and particularly so when the boys wrote home for their sleeping bags. The following persuasive letter from Ben was significant in gaining fuller approval from his parents.

Edinburgh
November 15, 1957

. . . We would much rather save the beauty of this countryside until springtime when it has a chance to show itself at its best. As for Scandinavia, it will not be any nicer in the spring than it is now—or, at least, not during the spring break which we have, which ends on April 14th. It is by far the *closest* place to go and if we go on student rates and stay in hostels (how you could ever think we would bury ourselves in the snow I don't know), it will cost us very little. We have contacts in Sweden, Marianne's folks plus some friends of George's. We are *not* planning to take the car. It would be much too expensive. Instead, we will drive as far as London where we will leave the car with the Wileys. From London we will take a train to Hamburg, Germany (costing only $10), and from there we will work our way easily enough to Copenhagen and across to Sweden. . . .

We have figured out the cost of our trip, and we make it to be at the outside no more than $75 or $80. If we stayed here in Edinburgh, we would spend twelve pounds or about $35 during the same three weeks period *just* for our boarding. Then we would have to buy our lunches out (the University will be closed) and this, plus extraneous expenses (seeing some Christmas shows), would probably run us a good $25 more. If we traveled during that time here in Britain, we'd probably spend as much, or more.

Ben's spirit was like a net that drew in for observation all that was read, felt and seen. The vitality of the Christian calling was becoming increasingly apparent. This was furthered not alone from the intellectual stimulation of New College, but in work with a group of under-privileged children in Greenside, a depressed section of the city. Many of the children were illegitimate. Earnestness of effort, prompted by their hard lot together with the excitements of intellectual ventures, are expressed in the following letter:

Edinburgh
November 18, 1957

Dear C_____:

Haven't we taken tremendous strides toward knowledge and control of our environment? True enough, and this is all well and good. The trouble is, we have become so literal-minded that we are unable to see beyond the barns of categories and types which we have built to hold our colossal harvest. We have become slaves of our own rational thought. We forget, in the exhilaration of discovery, that what we have come upon was there long before we came along. We act as if what we have is ours. Knowledge, however, is not possession; neither is it ever certain, except in a purely operational sense. If we find order in the world about us, we must remember that it is not derived from us. We have had nothing to do with making the world as it is and though we may at first think so, it is not something inherent in Nature herself; she did not "think" herself into this situation. For she is herself a "creature," even as we are creatures; and she derives from the same rational ground of Being as do we ourselves.

Another tangent, completely unpremeditated. But now a change of tune. I have begun to slide into the familiar routine of studying in odd half-hours between doing "more important things." I have gotten involved in the New College group and become chairman of the Department of Athletic Prowess in the Ancient Royal Order of The Knights of Greenside. This is a hectic affair—made up of teen-age kids in the slum district of Greenside here in Edinburgh. I am finding it really tough to communicate with them. There are five or six of us involved, and we are all new and unsure of ourselves. All I can say is that we are trying.

These youngsters die for Rock 'n Roll, and Elvis Presley is their God. It's one thing to try and work an interpretation of Christian life into the traditions of the Navajos. But, to me, it's stretching it to make Presley your mouthpiece for the Christian way of life. The important thing is trust, and we are trying to make them feel something of this, not only with us, but among themselves. It's not a pretty district, and they're up against it from the start. As far as my official title in the aforementioned "Royal Order," you will be proud to hear that I have become a real jock—as the say-

ing goes. We've started a boys' club—ages 8 to 12—with all the
frills. It's a cross between Cubs, Scouts, and the Y.M.C.A. We have
merit badges, categories of activities and appropriate titles—serf,
apprentice, Squire, and (holiest of holies) Knight—which can be
earned through fulfilling specific qualifications in each category.
Mine, as you have no doubt gathered, is the "Keep in Shape to
Defend Young Damsels in Distress" category. We have the use of
a dingy, bare-looking hall, and are starting completely from
scratch. It's going to be a lot of fun for all of us. . . .

A particularly potent letter is the following, in which the complex pieces in the kaleidescope seem to be falling more fully into
place:

Edinburgh
November 19, 1957

Dear N____:

Today has been an exceptional day. We rose reluctantly, shiv-
ered into our clothes, gulped our porridge, and set off for school.
Like two moles we rubbed our eyes and blinked up into the "daz-
zling" light of a patch of blue sky. The first sunshine we have seen
now for eleven days. Edinburgh, city of many moods, all of them
gray, had blushed and demurely shown herself in the light of day.
But now it's late afternoon—and I imagine tomorrow we will see
the end of such unnatural bliss.

I am still trying to catch a gleam of light before the sinking of
each sun. Every night we go to sleep and die a little; and every
morning we wake up and life begins anew. I believe that. It's the
old story of the natural cycle—life and death, rebirth and renewal.
There is a continual state of tension between what we are and
what we would be. There is the spirit in me that would live—that
cannot comprehend the nothingness of non-participation in the
world—and there is my body which will surely die. Our life is a
continual passing into death; but because we have a rational
awareness of the life which is momentarily ours, of the passionate
expectations of joy and fulfillment, we turn and try to swim
against the tide.

> "But is there any comfort to be found?
> Man is in love, and loves what vanishes,
> What more is there to say? . . ."

So says William Butler Yeats in one of his low moments. Poets
have been saying it for generations—Arnold, Wadsworth, Keats,

all of them. But they all fight against it too. Thomas put it best, I think (or, at least, I've been reading him a little lately, and he comes to mind). Forgive my dilettantism, by the way . . . I hate to quote things like this in letters, but I'm hoping you'll understand. Besides, I just came away this afternoon from a lecture on Dylan Thomas, so I hope my poetic musings may be excused.

> "Do not go gentle into that good night. . . ."
> (and)
> "Rage, rage against the dying of the light. . . ."

I know these words are far removed from the heart of the matter, as we know it deep down, somewhere in the pits of our stomachs, in the moments of despair and loneliness. I think, though, I shouldn't talk about the "pits of our stomachs," for that implies some kind of passionate feeling. It is the lack of this which is the really dreadful thing. We wake up one morning and find that we have become creatures of habit, that we really don't care about anything, that everything behind our eyes is dead, that everything we do and think and say is almost immediately turned to dust in our hands.

We can no longer speak glibly about the "progress" of civilization—about "better things for better living through science." The "world situation" which you refer to, is one in which we have been brought to a horrifying dead end. The possibility of complete and total physical destruction is now a buzzer on a control board, within easy reach of an outstretched hand. ICBMs are potentially "in the air," and suddenly everyone is frightened to death. I'm not throwing out a wholesale slap at "science"—the bug-a-boo of all "right-minded" and natural thinking folk. I'm not saying we should fall back on the twisted logic of the person who says that since man doesn't have wings, he isn't meant to fly.

Scientific achievement through the ages has been a projection of man's foremost natural blessing—that of rational thought. However, scientific achievement is not the only consequence from our gift for rational thought. Rational thought also gives us this agonizing sense of ourselves "in love with what vanishes."

The picture we have drawn for ourselves is incomplete; we have left ourselves out of it—not ourselves taken collectively; but ourselves taken individually, as personalities deriving their uniqueness not just from the environmental or historical situation in which we find ourselves, but from the inexplicable "give-ness" of our very individuality. I don't know if I am making this clear. . . .

I'd better say simply that *I think it is about time we came to our senses and gave a little more time and thought—not to the ICBM or to any deterrent to same . . . but to the problem of our own deepest nature. It is about time we realized what a miracle self-consciousness really is.*

It really comes down to the pre-eminent importance of our communicating with each other and with that part of us which we are forever trying to rediscover. I am convinced, "that it is Jesus Christ who has given us the 'Answer' to the needs and doubts at the heart of our being."

I'll simply say this: Jesus comes to you, and He says, "Follow me." He doesn't say you are now automatically "happy" or "secure" or that your troubles are over. What He does say is, "here is a new way to live your life—follow me." You think to yourself, "well, here's a ray of hope," and you follow. But you soon find out you cannot live up to the demands which Christ makes. It is impossible for us to follow the Sermon on the Mount. You can't, but Jesus did; and instead of trying to dub in any substitutes of our own (better things for better living through science), we ought to look at this moment in history where are met "the hopes and fears of all the years." It isn't a matter of theology as such, or even of "philosophy." It is a matter of belief and action arising from a demand which comes to every single one of us.

We can't be taken in by those who try to brush the whole thing aside by saying that Christ didn't exist. We have a great deal more data on the life of Christ than of Socrates, or even (if I'm not mistaken) Homer. People who do say this are begging the question. . . .

One thing is sure. If Christianity is all it's cracked up to be, we've got to begin making it the most important thing in the world. It needs to grow a lot taller than Church buildings. It needs to comprehend the total response of men to the situations and traditions in which they find themselves. It needs to realize (as did Christ) that the most fundamental response of man to the world about him is a religious response. It needs to extend its horizons far beyond the dear old country kirk, and certainly beyond the comfortable routine of suburbia, U.S.A. Millions of people in Asia and Africa with an annual income of less than $50. Millions dying every year through lack of nourishment and shelter. Who is going out to these people? The Christian Church had better begin taking account of its mission in the world. . . .

I am convinced . . . that we make very few decisions completely on our own. They come, I think, like "thieves in the night"; and in the morning we wake up and find we are possessed. . . .

A letter to his parents touches other areas of interest:

Edinburgh
November 23, 1957

Dear Mother and Dadden,

What I'm facing is the question of what I'm here for. The academic side is important for it puts me in touch with the background against which I must condition my own thought.

But I know, too, that I must work with people and that there is no better testing ground for this than the kinds with whom I am now working. They are rough and ready, grimy and dirty and full of an exuberant and undisciplined energy. . . . Their main trouble is that they seem to have no standards of values except those they manage to pick up in the streets and back alleys where they roam through all hours of the day and night. The potential, though, is great; and the kids are hungry for anything that can throw light on what their lives are supposed to mean. The problem is how to get through to them. You have to get across to them within the context of what they know. It's not easy. The first thing is to get to know them, and even this is hard to do.

This is what we're up against on Sunday nights. Then there is our Thursday Afternoon Club—"The Knights of Greenside" . . . I give them a workout with pushups, situps, cartwheels, head stands, etc. As soon as they join, they learn a little pledge which Bones whipped off one afternoon:

> "I am a Knight until I die
> When in my sepulchre I lie;
> For then My Master in the Sky
> Will judge my merit, low or high;
> But 'til that day on earth I'll stay,
> And serve all those who pass my way.
> I am a Knight until I die,
> Truth, Courage, Strength need I,
> Truth, Courage, Strength, for Aye!"

Bones has a real knack for this sort of thing. . . . Again, the kids are not particularly well mannered, and we have to really work to get them to do anything. There are some bright spots, however, and we have great hopes. No sooner do we show up than they are climbing all over our backs, yelling and screaming. They are full of energy and hungry for affection. A big job ahead.

I could really use a Double Quartet record. I have to take an arrangement off it to teach a makeshift singing group over here in time for our Christmas party on December 15th. . . .

Now, you've got to settle a current table dispute over here. We had prunes for dessert the other night—or at least what *I* call prunes. Everybody else maintained they were "plums." Now what do we call those things we have every now and then—not the wrinkled variety, but the kind of reddish ones with the skins all slack and all but falling off? If you have a tin of them around, you might take a look at the label (or even send it if it says prunes) and see whether it says "plums" or "prunes." I cannot emphasize how serious a matter this is. Until it is settled, we will rest in the "valley of indecision."

This is all a lot of foolishness, but because I told Mrs. Whitelaw I liked her "crunchies," you are now treated to the recipe for same:

I. 5 oz. rolled oats   3 oz. sugar
    3 oz. corn flakes   2 oz. margarine
    ½ tsp. bicarb of soda   1½ oz. lard
    1 tbsp. syrup   1 tsp. vanilla extract

II. Melt slowly in pan the margarine, lard, soda, and syrup; add dry ingredients and vanilla and mix well. Chuck it into a 2″ deep baking tin. Bake in slow oven 45 min. Cut while warm, but leave it in tin to cool.

This is one of the many goodies we gobble up almost daily. You might like to try it out or file it away for future reference.

And now before this letter becomes any more incoherent, I'd better sign off.

Love,

Goody

Letters to an athletics teammate, one to a cousin living in Dunfermline, and another to a young lady cover the gamut from "wanting to do more than there's time for"—to a moving experience of hearing Handel's *Messiah*.

Edinburgh
November 25, 1957

. . . It's going on 4:30 and the bluish haze of twilight is dissolving into more grayish tints. Night is settling in more quickly these days, and I can barely see across to the other side where lights are beginning to flicker against the silhouetted row of flats. . . .

Edinburgh
November 29, 1957

Dear Cousin C——,

Thanks so much for your letter.

I am sure you must have long since given up wondering what

has become of me. I must certainly apologize for my long silence since arriving here in Edinburgh.

Let me thank you for your invitation and say that I should like very much to visit you in Dunfermline. The name of this town has been ringing in my ears ever since I can remember. . . . A Saturday would be convenient—that is, if it is with you. I could easily come over on the train and spend the day and then go back in the evening.

Edinburgh
December 15, 1957

. . . Youth work is more time-consuming than I had anticipated. You can never let up, especially when you're in on the ground floor of something that is just getting under way, as I am in the Greenside Mission work. We are always racking our brains just to stay one jump ahead of the kids. I'm off down to the teenage group again tonight.

It will be another Rock 'n Roll session and it's my turn to do the little "epilogue" at the end. It will be quite a switch from our friend Elvis to the Gospel of St. Mark. I try to talk as naturally as possible, rather than "preach" about how they should run their lives. I am an outsider to their way of life, and it is pretty nervy of me to talk to them about what life ought to "mean" to them.

I have an awful lot to learn about putting myself across to people. Maybe it's because I'm so uncertain about who *I* am.

Somehow I've got to say, "Look, here's Jesus, He did this and this, He died for you, not because He had to, but because He loved us and so chose to sacrifice Himself. And because He was a man, He knows all about our fears and hopes and selfish desires. And He's looking at us, saying, 'Follow Me.' " What do you say? It's an awful lot to blurt out in one breath. Yet there it is.

. . . I went last night to hear Handel's *Messiah*. It was the first time I had heard the whole thing at once. The music is alive —the dramatic conflict between God and the world, with man caught in the middle, rejecting God, killing Him and yet, in the end, being gathered into the circle of His triumphant love.

If you have time over the Christmas break, you simply must hear it—in a live performance if possible. You will feel the passionate and exhilarating contrast in movement—the gambling glibness of the "All We Like Sheep" chorus, and the fury and passion of the baritone's "Why Do the Nations Rage So Furiously?" It is all there; the music projects the whole thing in the imagination and brings us right to the foot of the Cross.

A Christmas note was sent to a friend who had recently become engaged and who invited his counsel:

Dear G——,

So you've taken the great leap—Boy, that's great! Of course, I can't help thinking back nostalgically of the days with "the men," but . . .

As for teaming up with a Roman Catholic—I never knew before that Sue was one of "those" (I am in the heart of Knox-land, and the walls have ears). Seriously though, these are things which can only be worked out between the two people involved. I think "religion" is at the root of the human situation, whatever we may confess "with the top of our minds," as John Baillie says (pardon my erudite self). As far as ethics go, we don't need religion to teach us to "keep our hands out of our mothers' purses." Agnosticism is as much a religious "position" as Theism or any other "ism," and valid as long as it has been arrived at through "fear and trembling"—through an honest searching out of who we are.

What matters is the relationship between you and Sue, and your feeling of "rightness" for each other. . . . If "religion" is part of the relationship, then differences will matter; if it is not, then they won't matter. It's as simple as that—at least from my uninvolved view of things. At any rate, it's all good news to me. . . .

A letter to another friend is more than a simple thank-you note for a Christmas remembrance. Ben's love for this season can't be contained:

Edinburgh
December 18, 1957

Dear F——,

. . . Imagine my delight when I dragged myself home last night and found that monster package. The stocking is a work of art—it amazes me—and it hangs now with all its bulging promise in our "family" room, where we will gather tonight for a bit of Xmas cheer before "fjord-finder" Moses and I depart for faraway places. Such a bright and cheery stocking, with all its secrets hidden inside, is the work of no spur of the moment thought.

Though perhaps a little previous with my thanks (for we will soon be on the road and too numb to write a word), I want to let you know what a wonderful little Santa Claus worker you are —you and all your folks. . . .

As for carol singing, I'll be thinking of all the fun on Xmas

Eve—with the clear and frosty night, the shivering, snow flying, laughter and "Silent Night" and then "home again, home again" to a cup of hot chocolate and cheery fire—one of the "good tidings of life" which have been "added unto us" and stored in a treasury of memories.

I am beginning to find that my attraction for the ministry has had to do, not so much with any deep-seated, personal awareness of a Christian "call," as with a more basic desire for self-fulfillment and for association with the "good" as I have known it. . . . In the past, projected in little bits and pieces, I see the joy of to-getherness, the yearning for communion with another and with others, which is, it seems to me, the main theme of all our lives.

There is nothing more important than wanting and being wanted, and nothing more relevant to this miracle of communication than the Christian Gospel, where Christ comes to us and makes us come to Him, showing not only His mercy, but His power. (For when Jesus says "Follow me," there is no getting around an answer—we either follow or we don't; and if we don't then we deny ourselves; for what is miraculous about Jesus is not so much that He is God, but that He is man—"Everyman," identifying himself with man as he is and with man as he would be—the triumph of one over the other—the demand which is always before man simply because man is what he is—created by God and in dynamic relation with God.)

What I am fighting against really is the idea of playing a role. . . . I cannot lose sight of the distinction between the "me" I know myself to be and the "me" I must be to be a minister. It is a matter of being too self-conscious to lose myself in a selfless role. And I am no exhibitionist. But these are all abstractions divorced from the "heart of the matter"—the rationale, I suppose, of one who is as yet afraid to dare. But enough—If I keep on this way you will think I am groveling in the depths of despair. Well, I'm not. Exams are out of the way, and Bones and I will soon strap on our snowshoes and go off in search of a misplaced aurora borealis. . . .

It is now after our little "family gathering," and I must tell you that nary a crumb remains of those crunchy, delicious and perfectly intact toll house cookies. The lollipops are safely stored in our knapsack—and as for that last little something in the foot of the stocking, all I can say is that you are one jump ahead of the St. Bernards; and I can't wait for the first warming nip in a frosty Nordic hostel. Thanks once again, F., to you and R. and all your wonderful family for such a cheery bit of Xmas thought. And I hope this finds you all well and in the best of Holiday Spirits.

Ben's pristine honesty, tender sensitiveness and devotion are seen in a further letter written at his last Christmas:

Edinburgh
December 16, 1957

Dear Mother and Dadden:

I hope this finds you enjoying the warmer climes of New Orleans. By the time you read this, I will be envying you the warmth of a "tropical" Christmas. If you are reading this where anyone else is around—to whom I should be remembered—please give them all my best and say that I am thinking of them.

If there is one good thing about being away from home on Christmas, it is the way you come to remember, as you never have before, how really close you are to all things familiar and familial. This is really a time of remembrance—to recall or to imagine again all the moments of togetherness sprinkled over the years that have passed so quickly.

It is not all just a sentimental remembrance of "happy times gone by." The last thing I want to do is sink into this kind of dreamy, self-indulgent emotion. We cannot live in the past, or we will never get anything done in the here-and-now. If there is one thing I have learned from our energetic selves, it is the importance of getting on with the job at hand. Every moment of our lives is a commitment, and we are responsible for the fulfillment of these commitments. But, if this is so, we are committed as well to the past and the tradition which has formed us. . . .

When I look back, it is to recall the love and care—the "always being there"—that I have known in you both ever since I can remember; and, having known such love, it is for me now to live it and to live *up* to it and to pass it on to others. I know now that the most important thing in life is to love and be loved; and I mean it when I say the primary way I know this is through knowing you both together as "Mother and Dadden" and the love which you have made the primary element in all our family life. These are all the things which I wanted to somehow say before I left; but I am glad I waited until now.

It is for me now to decide what I am going to do with my life; but, whatever I do, I know wherein my life is grounded and to whom I owe this grounding.

Friday night the overseas students (almost all of whom are American) threw a Christmas party for all of New College and, as part of the program, set the stage for a very important theological debate between Principal John Baillie and Professor James Stewart on the one hand and Professors McIntyre and McEwen on the other. The subject, to which they brought all of their faith and wisdom, was "The Existence or Non-Existence of Santa Claus." Principal Baillie put forth a very convincing "pro" argument, based on the ontological evidence. Professor McIntyre "rebutted" with an attack upon what he called the "Prima Clausa" argument point of view; and while Professor Stewart relied upon his weighty argument of silence, Professor McEwen proceeded to deliver a devastating attack upon the "Papist myth of St. Nicholas." The moderator (an instructor in Hebrew and Old Testament, who had scrounged a pretentious looking rabbi's beard from somewhere or other) tipped the scales in favor of those arguing "for" the existence of venerable Father Christmas. It was an awfully good party. It is so seldom we have a chance to mingle together as a community. And this time I helped said mingling along by squiring one of the Scots lassies I work with down in Greenside. She is a good dancer—we had a lot of fun. . . .

With all of the study and with the insight and faith of the men with whom I am in daily contact, my faith becomes every day more real and alive. I know more surely that the meaning of life is contained in the coming of Jesus—in the Cross and in the Resurrection—in the giving that is receiving, in the life-long seeking after self-fulfillment that can only be found through our giving and thus receiving from another.

There is nothing more dismaying than to run across a minister who should not be a minister. I am convinced that this is no decision which I can make by myself; and yet I know that the day is rapidly approaching when the decision will have to be made. I know only this—that I will not, indeed cannot, go into the ministry unless I am literally forced to do it. God has not yet chosen me to be a minister, and, unless He does, I cannot argue myself into playing a role that I am not meant to play. I know, too, of course, that I cannot afford to shut my ears to a call which may very well be forthcoming. My state of mind is, to say the least, unsettled. And perhaps in a way it will always be; I doubt if we are ever "sure" of many of the things we do. . . . I am giving up trying to analyze and pick apart my every passing fancy (or at least so I tell myself). It is a tormenting and self-indulgent habit. I simply try to act these days according to the "given-ness" of those things to which I seem somehow responsible in the moment. . . .

You will be interested to know, if you don't know already, that the Symon family seems to have come originally from a little town by the name of Milnethort, about thirty miles north west of Dunfermline. It seems there is an old graveyard there full of Symon tombstones from quite a way back. Sometime in the spring I'm going to take Chris and Peter for a run up there to see some of them. Peter gave me all he had (which was quite a bit) on the family tree, and I've got it traced back. We also came across the old newspaper clipping, the obituary of one Sir Josiah H. Symon (K.C., K.C.M.G.) (King's Council and Knight Commander of St. Michael and St. George), "a Scotsman who played a distinguished part in Australian affairs." I have the article copied out. He was a lawyer who became Attorney General of Australia and was one of the framers of the Commonwealth Constitution. So, what do you think of that? . . .

We have checked on hostels and there is a good string of them open along the main route and also a good line of student houses. We will hitchhike from Hamburg to Lubeck, where we will take a boat across to Copenhagen. . . .

There should be some shortbread arriving down there sometime, tho' perhaps not in time for Christmas. . . .

                                                        Goodie

Ben and George Moses planned a Christmas party for the youngsters at Greenside. His fellow students said they never saw anyone happier than Ben at that party—laughing, dancing, and singing with the youngsters and giving them Christmas treats. Ben felt so deeply for the love-starved children at Greenside that he was considering taking a room where he could live among them.

Mrs. Whitelaw was up early in the morning to give them a hot breakfast for the jaunt to London. With a final warning to guard the heavy traffic, they were off. She reported later, "I never saw them so happy."

About fifty miles outside of London, on the great North Road, the most travelled in England, a negligent driver had left his low-bedded truck, loaded with protruding steel bars, standing in the middle of the road. The truck had a flat tire, but was allowed to stay in the road, without attendance or light as night approached.

The haze and early darkness blended the grey color and low level of the truck until it could not be observed except at close distance. Ben saw the truck but not soon enough. His wheels were turned. The brake was on—but it was too late. Both young men were instantly killed.

Mrs. Whitelaw found the following note, together with a Christmas remembrance, after the young men had left:

Dear Mrs. Whitelaw and Douglas,

Just to say "Cheerio" and thanks for all the last minute scrounging about for our benefit—mail, sandwiches, and a general sharing of our rush of the moment.

As I sift through some of the odds and ends in our room, I ran across these two library books which are due back just about now. I am sorry to ask you, but I wonder if either of you might have time to drop them off along George IV Bridge? I should certainly appreciate it.

Well, we are out of your hair for a while—chance now for you to catch a rest.

Have a good Holiday, and we will be thinking about you as we trek across the frozen wastes of Sweden's glaciers. In fact, we'll probably be thinking very fondly of this warm little hearth.

So long for now,

Ben and George

P.S. Here's some more tinfoil—the last of the lot.

What might they have talked about on the drive from Edinburgh toward London? The topics would have been endless. The place of poetry and religion! The oneness that there ought to be between faith and life! Their reaction to speculative theology; the necessity for a man ever to stay on the quest of finding and knowing himself; and, most likely of all, there would have been an expression of a deeper confidence that the only way was in the steps of Jesus, the Christ.

CHAPTER 7

"The Next Adventure"

$\mathbf{M}$RS. SYMON wrote of the last rites held for her son:

"On December 29, 1957, the church, where Ben first felt the challenge of Christ's ministry and which blessed his decision to enter seminary was filled to standing overflow. The community that had loved him came bowed in grief. His casket was placed in the chancel before the jeweled cross which symbolized to Ben the meaning to life here and the hope for life eternal.

"As Ben's close friends of high school and college filled the front pews as honorary pallbearers, the winter sun, through the magnificent window in the chancel, made a soft glow over all. The service emphasized the triumph of life over death in hymns which Ben had loved and sung in pew and choir. In the Scriptures came the assurances of God's mercy and the promise of eternal life in Christ. After a prayer of thanksgiving for the good Ben gave the world, the organ pealed forth with Handel's 'Hallelujah' of which Ben wrote feelingly in a letter posted the day before his death."

The window to which Mrs. Symon refers shows, in its upper panel, the glory of the Risen Christ. The panel beneath portrays the Savior on the Cross. These symbols undoubtedly said to many, "Ben Symon's spirit lives on."

It lives on in many memorials. Gifts from parents and friends here and abroad made possible the establishment of the Benjamin Goodall Symon, Jr. Fellowship Fund at Amherst. The income from the fund annually assists a graduating senior who desires to fit himself for Christian service.

Fraternity brothers built a "typing room" in the Chi Psi Lodge equipped with typewriters and other equipment for the preparation of assignments. On the wall are pictures of Ben and George and a memorial plaque.

An anonymous donor planted a copper beech tree on the campus in Ben's memory.

The spring concert of sacred music by the Amherst Choir was sung as a memorial to Ben. One special number, "Give Rest, O Christ," was dedicated with particular feeling to Ben. The majestic words reached out to ennoble many a heart:

"Give rest, O Christ, to Thy servants with Thy saints, where sorrow and pain are no more, neither sighing, but life everlasting. Thou only art immortal, the Creator and Maker of man, and we are so mortal, formed of the earth, and unto the earth shall we return: for so Thou didst ordain, when Thou createdst me, saying, Dust thou art, and unto dust shalt thou return. All we go down to the dust; and, weeping o'er the grave, we make our song. Alleluia! Alleluia! Alleluia!"

Scottish children in Greenside sent a floral piece to the Bronxville Church with an accompanying card, reading, "To Uncle Ben."

Students at the University of Edinburgh pooled their funds and sent a contribution to the Benjamin Goodall Symon, Jr. Fellowship at Amherst.

The simple Bronxville cemetery where Ben is buried was established more than a century ago by a vigorous Scottish congregation. Azaleas planted over Ben's grave came as a gift from a friend in Sweden. Several other plantings are memorials to him. It is compatible ground for him. There one feels eternity, the beauty of life's simplicities, and the truth—"Though dead they yet speak."

Collection plates inscribed to his memory are used each Sunday in the "Youth Chapel" service of the Bronxville Church, where he preached his only sermon.

Books in the library of that Church and a dogwood tree on its lawn memorialize his love of literature and nature.

The Hipwah Christian Missionary School in Hong Kong received funds for teaching equipment, in Ben's memory.

These are tangible matters: a scholarship, offering plates, and a typing room in a fraternity house. But they are symbolic of the influence from Ben Symon's life.

His life and death inspired many young people to direct their lives toward spiritual ends. That influence, like snow on a wide landscape, goes on adding to the good growth in the world. It is conveyed in their letters to Ben's parents:

> Every once in a while, I think or say something—and then suddenly realize, "Why, that's Ben's."
> I think he would have liked that.—His influence did not and *will not* fade out.

> My meeting your son and being with him is so fresh and vivid that, even now, I can feel again the delight of listening to his honest reflections; watching the changing expressions on his face, from seriousness to boyish gaiety; that heart-melting friendliness of his—so direct and genuine.

> Ben and George are one step ahead of the rest of us. Now they are beginning a new life. It is only when I think this way that I find peace with God and myself. I hope that both of you have found this peace.

> Every time I succeed in being tolerant and patient and kind— those qualities which characterized Ben—and yes, when I'm absent-minded—a little bit that he has irrevocably left, will be living.

> My first reaction was that a grave injustice had been done, that youth had been cheated. But we who knew what Ben stood for in his strong, unpretentious way, cannot but feel that in his death there was victory.
> Ben lived his life as if it were a prologue to an eternal drama, and I feel that mysterious drama is far from ended.

The Edinburgh chapter, though brief in terms of time, left a deep and an abiding influence in many lives. These letters to Mr. and Mrs. Symon reflect that influence:

> All of us who study and search and try, feebly by his example, to find and do God's will, have been and are still continually heartened and helped by him.
> Young people clamoured for Ben and clung to him and he went out of his way to help them. To know Ben was to love him. You can be justly proud of Ben's memory and if this is an example of the youth of America, you have indeed a proud heritage.

> He will always live in my heart. I never knew a more dependable friend, and I shall always respect his strength of mind and character.

Ben is still living and my spiritual inheritance from him is immeasurable.

One of the respected names in Scotland and America is Professor James S. Stewart of Edinburgh University, who wrote:

Ben showed himself to be a most alert and promising student. He had been to our home for an evening, and my wife was so glad to be able to entertain him. God will use these young lives in even greater ways than He could have done on earth. You will have the comfort of knowing that we do not really lose our dear ones who go over to the immortal side of death. They are our daily comrades still, and we are going to see them again by and by.

The police took from Ben's pocket the Testament given by his mother the night before he left home, its pages now stained with his blood. In his wallet they found two worn cards. One contained the words of a prayer of St. Francis. The other was a "prayer guide" distributed by the Bronxville Church more than a year before. Each must have been referred to daily for many months.

Among his papers was found a prayer which he wrote for the 1953 Service held at the Bronxville Reformed Church just at Easter dawning.

Almighty and everlasting God, on this glorious Easter morning, commemorating the triumphant victory of Thy Son over all mortal power—even the power of death—we thank Thee for the great gift Thou hast bestowed on us: the gift of Jesus Christ, that through the agony He endured for us we may achieve eternal life, and that our own wrongdoing may be redeemed in Thy sight. We bow before Thee in acknowledgment that there is no greater gift than this.

We cry out to become a part of His triumph. Strengthen our faith, broaden it, deepen it, build it up—make it a solid block which will withstand onslaughts of crisis and change.

Grant that through such a faith we may realize more fully the glory and the mystery of our Savior's Resurrection.

Hear our prayers, O God, for we pray in the name of our Lord, Jesus Christ. Amen.

May Ben's faith, expressed that morning, give to you, as it did to him, a resilience and nobility that this world can never give nor take away!